A Weekend
Memoir

A Weekend
Memoir

by Ernest Hillen

OXFORD
UNIVERSITY PRESS

OXFORD
UNIVERSITY PRESS

70 Wynford Drive, Don Mills, Ontario M3C 1J9
www.oupcanada.com

Oxford University Press is a department of the University of Oxford.
It furthers the University's objective of excellence in research, scholarship,
and education by publishing worldwide in

Oxford New York

Auckland Cape Town Dar es Salaam Hong Kong Karachi
Kuala Lumpur Madrid Melbourne Mexico City Nairobi
New Delhi Shanghai Taipei Toronto

With offices in
Argentina Austria Brazil Chile Czech Republic France Greece
Guatemala Hungary Italy Japan Poland Portugal Singapore
South Korea Switzerland Thailand Turkey Ukraine Vietnam

Oxford is a trade mark of Oxford University Press
in the UK and in certain other countries

Published in Canada by Oxford University Press

Library and Archives Canada Cataloguing in Publication

Hillen, Ernest, 1934–
A weekend memoir / written by Ernest Hillen ; introduction by Roy MacGregor.

Stories first published in the early 1970s in Weekend magazine.

ISBN 978-0-19-542992-3

1. Canada—Biography. 2. Canada—History. I. Title.
II. Title: Weekend magazine.

FC626.A1H54 2008   971.009'9   C2008-903960-2

Cover image: "Late Summer Harvest," Prince Edward Island. Marilyn Trenchard Photography.

Oxford University Press is committed to our environment. This book is printed on
Forest Stewardship Council certified paper which contains 30% post-consumer waste.
Printed and bound in Canada.

1 2 3 4 – 12 11 10 09

Printed on 30%
recycled paper

6
trees were saved
for our forests

Preserving our environment
Oxford University Press Canada chose to use recycled
paper to print this book and saved these resources[1]:

energy	water	greenhouse gases	solid waste
30 million BTUs	55,227 L	2035 lbs	781 kg

Printed by **Webcom Inc.**
on Legacy TB Natural 30% post-consumer waste.

FSC

Mixed Sources
Product group from well-managed
forests, and recycled wood or fiber

Cert no. SW-COC-002358
www.fsc.org
© 1996 Forest Stewardship Council

[1]Estimates were made using the Environmental Defense Paper Calculator.

Table of Contents

Acknowledgements

A t the time, a few of us actually knew they were our "good old days." Now and then we even told each other so, "These are the good old days *right now!*" We were, simply, very aware of our extraordinary luck to be working at *Weekend Magazine* in Montreal. That was 40 years ago, and magazine journalism in this country was, perhaps, at the peak of its form. For me, it was one long adventure, so exciting, so absorbing, that sometimes it seemed I was living like a person in a book, an imaginary person.

"We" were a handful of editors and writers—Jacqui Bishop, Wayne Clark, James Quig, Paul Rush, Robert Stall, Patricia Welbourne—who seemed to connect a lot. And always, always, we talked stories; stories were the heart of everyday matter. There were many other interesting and agreeable men and women on *Weekend's* sizeable staff (writers alone numbered 14), but I remember those six the best, almost as a little club. My membership lasted from mid-1967 to early 1974.

Besides the friendships, I recall how much each of them, not always knowingly either, taught me in his or her inimitable way— about listening, about observing, and about thinking. Important stuff for anyone working at writing. All these years later, I remain indebted to all six.

I do want to single out Paul Rush, our managing editor. There were editors above Paul, but gifted with his quick wit, elephantine memory, and superb editorial instincts, it was he who really ran the magazine. A trait of his that helped me a lot, and everybody else, of course, was his general openness to ideas (not so common among editors) and then his skill in selecting the useful ones and nimbly shaping them into story ideas—the platinum of magazines. Paul later carried on distinguished careers in journalism and in teaching journalism in Toronto.

And most of all, there were all the fascinating Canadians across this fabulous Canada who, with much grace, allowed me to listen, observe, and participate a little in their lives. To this day I remain in their debt as well. It was easy to grow fond of them and so, like a pirate, I carried away with me not only their stories but also those rich affections. After each encounter, I felt I'd left a bit of myself behind, too.

And, finally, to the present. I'd like to thank David Stover, the imaginative president of Oxford University Press Canada who reached out to bring these stories to a new audience; Jennie Rubio, editor, whose deft managing of the project made it what it is; and my wife, Marta Tomins, who as always, is both my in-house editor and my life's joy.

Cambridge, Ontario
June, 2008

Foreword

BY ROY MacGREGOR

Ernest Hillen has the hands of a concert pianist. They have long and slender fingers, nails hard as maple and always, always perfectly trimmed and cleaned. They seem entirely out of synch with the profession.

Writers are rarely noted for their hands—though Sherwood Anderson did write brilliantly of a pair in his 1919 classic *Winesburg, Ohio*—and, if they are noticed at all, it is because the nails are bitten to the quick, because they are forever fidgeting, because they are black from carbon paper or brown-stained by nicotine.

But not Ernest Hillen's hands. They are as calm and unblemished as the man who controls them at the keyboard. They are, most appropriately, more like those of a pianist, for the best comparison I can make to Hillen's life work is that he writes as if he were one of those rare and gifted humans who can play by ear, perfectly. He hits exactly the right notes without ever seeming to try. He can slow words down or speed them up, seemingly at will, and he writes with a rhythm that is, at all times, captivating. It is not loud. There is absolutely nothing of the show-off in him— none of that "Look, Ma, *no hands!*" style that afflicts so many of our more literary fiction writers. His writing is like the man himself: straightforward, honest, interested, and soft-spoken, but with hidden power. His writing is great company—but then, so, too, is the man.

Consider for a moment a single line from the story included here on his visit to the Stony Rapids reserve in Northern

Saskatchewan: "For the last five years, there have been no slow deaths for men." It takes a moment for meaning to settle in, but then, suddenly, the imagination is released. Why would that be? What sorts of "fast" deaths is he talking about? He has used only a dozen words, but the reader turns them into a dozen pages, fully illustrated.

It takes a fine hand to craft such minimal-yet-evocative sentences. Perhaps it is partly in the genes, for Ernest comes from a family that, through five generations carved fine furniture in Amsterdam. His father, also a builder, worked for the Royal Ontario Museum after coming to Canada, designing and setting up exhibition galleries. Ernest builds with words and, as these essays so wonderfully demonstrate, he builds to last.

I don't know when I first met Ernest. Likely at *Maclean's*, or perhaps when he was a senior editor at *Saturday Night*, but I had already known him for years by reputation alone. Naturally, I didn't much care for him. It's a common affliction among the young, the ambitious and the insecure who cannot comprehend why someone else has what they so desperately want for themselves. But I was very young and just starting out in magazines—I was in charge of the "slush" fund at Maclean's, reading the hundreds of unsolicited manuscripts that flooded in to the then monthly, and responding to them by writing "A," "B," "C," "D," etc. on the top of each one so the secretaries could send back a "Dear ____, Thank you for sending us your recipe for Saskatoon berry pie, but Maclean's, unfortunately...."—and what I desperately wanted was a job like the staff-writer job Ernest Hillen had at *Weekend* magazine.

Ernest then was among a dozen or so prolific, brilliant, often eccentric, full-time, salaried writers for what were known as the weekend supplements. They were cheap, thin rotogravure publications that the competing newspaper chains in the country used to attract Saturday readers—there being then no Sunday publications in Canada.

The *Star Weekly* had been around since before the First World War, but the heyday of the weekend supplements was during the 1960s and 1970s, when *Weekend* magazine, which dated back to 1951, went up each Saturday against *The Canadian* magazine, a relatively new supplement created by the Southam chain of newspapers and the *Toronto Star*. At the time of their greatest circulation in those years, *Weekend* and *The Canadian* were reaching four million readers a week—an absolutely astonishing market penetration by today's standards.

I wanted a writing job like Ernest Hillen had over at *Weekend*. I wanted his job because he got to travel all over the country and visit fascinating places. And I wanted the job Earl McRae had over at *The Canadian*, because Earl got to write long fascinating pieces about sports personalities. Naturally, I was jealous of him, too. Little did I realize that, very shortly, Don Obe would leave *Maclean's* to take up the editorship of *The Canadian* and would then hire me—only to become fast and lifelong friends with Earl. Same thing happened with Ernest.

The bylines of those times stand large in memory. The humour of Tom Alderman, the gentle brilliance of David Cobb, the breathtaking talents of Marci McDonald and Walter Stewart, the hilarious antics of Earl McRae, who once pretended to be the managing editor and told Phil Esposito, who had phoned to complain about a piece done by McRae, that "Mr McRae, unfortunately, passed away suddenly on the weekend"—a conversation that ended with Earl receiving condolences from the very man he had so upset.

There were so many other great talents at both magazines. There were the staff writers, only a handful of whom are mentioned above, and the various editors—hell, in our copy department alone we had Anne Collins, now publisher of Random House, and Margaret Wente, now the *Globe*'s marquee columnist. *The Canadian* was produced out of Toronto while *Weekend* was Montreal-based. We were more into Canadian personalities and, in particular, sports profiles, whereas over at *Weekend* editors like Paul Rush and John Macfarlane were chasing ambitious stories all over the world, and had great talents like James Quig, Pat Nagle, Michael Posner, and, of course, Ernest Hillen.

Paul Rush believes Ernest had such success with profiles because "he has a most receptive ear. He actually listens to people and the more he listens the more they tend to talk to him. They realize that Ernest actually wants to know them and who they are and how they live their lives. Indeed, he has stayed in touch with some of his subjects over the years, though I doubt he would call them 'subjects.'"

Paul says Ernest was one who had to "talk" out his stories—my own preference, I should add here, is to not say a single word about a story until it is finished—and the favoured place for both coming up with the idea and "talking out" the story once the research had been completed was the old Queen's Hotel bar in downtown Montreal.

"It was so old that the bar of leather and dark wood had buttons at most of the booths," Paul remembers. "And when you wanted service you pressed a button and a number would flip up by the bartender. Two or three of us would sit around and say 'what about a story on...' and eventually we would define the area and Ernest would pack his notebook and set off. My instructions were usually along the lines of: 'Ernest, find a family farm and write about it.' And Ernest would go off and do a people story bolstered with a few facts. He had the skill—which most lack—to make that type of story shine."

The magazines did not last. Cigarette and car advertising left for television. Production costs rose. The six-week lag time between going to print and publication—inconceivable in today's world of instant news and comment—stretched far too long. And most significantly of all, the newspaper wars went into a convenient ceasefire where competing papers in the same city had no need of supplement attraction—if, indeed, there was any competition to be found.

Much of that work does not survive the test of time. Much of my own material seems terribly dated now as I look back on it. But, curiously, Ernest Hillen's does not. Perhaps it is because Ernest, more so than any of us writing in those days, stayed relatively clear of headline events and front-page personalities, and devoted himself, instead, to ordinary people in an extraordinary country. Their stories are as alive and valid today as they were the day he dropped off his neatly typed manuscripts in the editor's office.

He had the ability to deliver a story as big as the entire country —a journey across Canada in the dead of winter—or as small as having a very minor role in murder. (You'll have to read that one —but watch your neck.) He could write one week about the King of Rodeo Riders and the next about a soon-to-vanish lighthouse keeper on the coast.

Ernest is a watcher. His work—the attention to detail, the sense of being there without being the slightest bit intrusive—reminds me of a Jack Hodgins' short story, "The Leper's Squint." Hodgins' narrator, a writer, is visiting Ireland in search of inspiration and finds it when he stops at the Rock of Cashel, and a guide shows him a small opening in the rocks were the outcasts were allowed to watch, but not participate in, the great ceremonies of the day. It was, Hodgins writes, "Like looking through the eye of a needle," the observers privy to the scene and the sounds, but not quite a part of it. That is how I see Ernest: the face on the other side of the window, carefully taking down notes.

"Memory," Hillen once wrote, "is, finally, all we own." It is how he ended his magnificent memoir *The Way of a Boy*—the story of his childhood in a Japanese internment camp following the invasion of Indonesia, where Hillen's Dutch family had lived and worked on a tea plantation. He was eight years old when he was taken to the camp, where he spent a grueling three-and-a-half years in a prison where one out of every five detainees, including Ernest's very best childhood friend, died before liberation.

Ernest Hillen's ability to convey sense of place and meaning was what turned *The Way of a Boy* into a bestseller and saw it translated into several other languages around the world, including Japanese. Mordecai Richler praised Hillen for "the clear, honest voice" that makes this book, and a subsequent memoir, *Small Mercies*, such compelling reading. And it is that crystal clear and honest voice that is on display here in twenty-two different magazine pieces from the glory years of the weekend supplements.

Hillen takes us from the inner workings of a passionate family bookstore in Toronto—where his own mother found work after the family emigrated to Canada—to the burdens of a small-town newspaper editor out West. He goes trapping with a fascinating man who has spent the last 40 years in the wilderness of Northern Ontario. He visits fish workers on their isolated Gulf Island where work takes up two months of the year and wild gossip the other ten. He rides the Bistro train to Montreal—"the only way to fly"— and rides the streets of small town Ontario with the local police chief. The ordinary Canadians captured here range from cursing rodeo heroes to hell-and-brimstone evangelists, yet all seem extraordinary at the hands of Ernest Hillen.

"There is such an incredible humanism about his writing," says Jennie Rubio, his editor at Oxford University Press, "really an unusual feel for all the different textures that make up people's lives."

And those people, you will shortly see, couldn't be in better hands.

———◆◆◆———

[NOTE: Multiplying dollar numbers in this book by 5 gives a rough sense of their current value.]

To Maia Hillen
for love and laughter

Chapter 1

"The Old Ways Are Fading Away"

The black dog stops barking and sits down on the gravel driveway watching me. Nothing stirs in the house or around the barn. Crickets sound off in the heat of late August [1969] and the hum of insects swells up from the grass and bushes. I am not opening the door of the taxi until somebody comes and gets that dog away.

Minutes pass. I'm having my first lesson about life in the country: there's almost never a need for hurry.

The screen door on the side of the house opens. The dog wanders off; Toots is her name, I learn later. A lady is standing on the porch, a halo of tight grey curls around her head—my hostess, Jeanne (pronounced Jeannie) Coulchard. She looks closely at this city person. I had tried to explain my mission to her over the phone from Montreal—a few days' visit to try to catch some of the mood of farm living—but it was a good thing that agricultural representative W.N.T. Ashton had already set it up for me. Ashton works out of Stratford, Ontario, and I am on this farm, four miles south of there, on his recommendation.

Jeanne suggests I go down to the barn where her husband is busy with a new calf. They knew the calf was coming, she explains, but the mother jumped the gun yesterday and had it right in the field.

Norman Coulchard doesn't seem busy at all. He's just standing there with his youngest son Alex, 14, watching their calf wobbling about in its stall. I tell him I wanted to come yesterday but was held up. Now it's nearly noon. His pale blue eyes look me over slowly.

"Well, now, that doesn't matter at all," he says finally. "There's six days next week not used yet."

This is the 100th year Coulchards have been farming in Perth County, Ontario. Norman is 60 and farming is the "only trade I ever knew." Until 1967 he worked 100 acres. Then he bought a 120-acre spread adjoining his. One day, the oldest son, Gordon, 30, may run it when he finds himself a wife, but for now the two are operated as a single unit. Norman has about 90 head of cattle, most of them Holsteins. Thirty-five are mature milking cows, others are young males fed out for beef, and there are some heifers kept for replacement. He feeds about 30 pigs and 50 chickens. This year about 80 acres stood in grain, 45 in hay, 15 in corn, 60 in pasture, and there are 20 acres in bush.

Norman and Alex are showing me a clutch of three-day-old kittens sucking away at their mother, when Jeanne rings the bell for dinner.

<hr />

Six calendars and a red electric clock decorate the kitchen walls. The plastic tablecloth features bunches of red and pink roses. To the side is an immense wood-burning stove not used in summer. Norman says he bought it in 1942.

"I couldn't get $2 for it now. But it saves a bit on the oil, and when you're sitting by it in winter, you know, you're just as warm as warm."

I meet Gordon now and Winston, 29. Both live and work on the farm. Larry, 24, also lives home, but he has a full-time job delivering mink feed to mink ranches. He would like to farm, too, but there just isn't enough work for an extra man right now. The only one not at home is Norma, Gordon's twin, who is married to farmer Fred Howe, and lives a few miles away.

Norman says a short prayer and this is what we eat: sweet corn picked this morning, sliced tomatoes still warm from the sun, cucumber and onion salad, cabbage salad, boiled potatoes, boiled beets, cold ham, two kinds of bread, homemade pickles, cut-up peaches that have stood in sugar, sweet buns, and strawberry pie.

The radio is on for news and weather. Stanley Burke has taken leave of absence from reading the CBC news to join a church campaign to try to end the suffering in Biafra. They know him from watching TV in winter. In summer, they hardly turn it on at all. Except for Johnny Cash.

Across the top of Norman's balding head runs a three-inch scar. After chores one night in the early 1920s, he was fooling around the swimming hole with friends. He was chased and dove into the shallow end. "Saw stars like on a winter's night," he recalls. "I climbed out and stood on the bank with the blood running down to my toes. My friends got me to the doctor in St Mary's and he bandaged me up like an Arab."

Somehow a few flies got in the kitchen. When dinner is done Gordon has swatted each of them dead with a copy of *The Western Ontario Farmer*.

◆━◆━◆

The hot air hangs over the field. There's no wind. Norman and I are straightening a stretch of barbed-wire fence by the creek. With a sledgehammer he slams the steel stakes into the dry ground, pulls the coiling wire tight, and twists it secure. There's not a drop of sweat on his face. I hammer in a stake and I'm wet through in a minute.

"Only once," he replies when I ask if he's ever in his life been really angry with someone. "And him I didn't like much to start with. But anger is only one letter away from danger, you know. I've never even given one of the boys a licking."

We sit down in the grass. "The old ways are more or less fading away," he tells me. "You cared about community life then, you harvested together. Now everybody is on their own. You don't know your neighbours 'cause there's no reason to know them. Cars have made a lot of changes, too. These days the young can go so *far*....

"I don't understand the human race. All this money to go up to the moon. It would've been better spent inventing a tap to put on a cow so you could turn her milk on and off when you wanted.

"They say a fella can't farm without an education today. Well, now, I say he can—if the fella with the education leaves him alone."

When we get back to the pick-up truck on the road, Frank Thom, the electrician, is parked alongside waiting with a bill for $8.45. He hands it over saying it's for $845.

"This here fella...Ernie Hilton," Norman introduces me, "is up here from Montreal to kinda, well, you know, find out about farming."

Frank Thom shakes hands gravely.

—◦◦◦◦—

After evening chores, everybody has washed and changed clothes, and gathered in the parlour where the piano is. Norma and Fred and their three small children are visiting. In the next two hours I am treated to orangeade and raisin cookies and family deliberations on Alex going to high school next week, neighbours, hitchhikers, relatives, bee stings, the grandchildren, other neighbours, a highway accident involving a dog and a cement truck, mini skirts, Mennonite farmers who don't use electricity, and whether or not we're going to the annual fall fair in Mitchell tomorrow. I am asked the only two direct questions during my stay there: what church do you belong to? Are you married? Alex shows me his collections of 102 pencils from different places and 170 match folders, and Jeanne brings out her collection of coffee spoons.

Alex won a prize in public speaking last winter and now he recites the speech. It's about the history and ways of money. He starts off saying if you had a billion dollars you could buy 500,000 cars, which would stretch bumper to bumper from Halifax to Toronto.

At midnight I'm upstairs in the big soft bed in the guest room. A car goes by on the highway and I can hear it a long, long time.

—◦◦◦◦—

The fields and trees are in mist. The moon is still in the sky. A grey cat sits cleaning itself in front of the barn. In back the cows are waiting. Chore time.

The Coulchards know their tasks. Nobody gives orders. The big job is milking. Feed and hay is distributed, milking machines are washed; then the doors are opened for the cows. The awkward beasts come clattering in, udders swinging, bawling, and each makes straight for her own stall. Warmth spreads through the barn and with it that powerful smell. The generator isn't on yet and for a moment there's only the sound of tails swatting and Holsteins eating, their tongues swishing in the grain. It's a soft sound, like murmuring water.

Before the milking machine is set onto a cow, her teats are washed with hot water and an antiseptic solution. This is for purposes of hygiene. But she also "lets down" better then, explains Larry, who helps with chores before going to work. I see that some immediately start dripping, and with one the milk is actually squirting out.

What each cow gives is weighed and noted and then dumped into the stainless steel milk cooler. All the milking equipment is kept spotlessly clean.

Everybody is working but there doesn't seem to be anything I'm able to do. It occurs to me that if I really had to earn my keep I would have to be adept at the skills of an animal nutritionist, a veterinarian, a carpenter, a mechanic, a soil expert, a weather forecaster, a financier, a chemist, and an accountant. Every farmer is, or should be.

When all the cows are milked, they are herded along the walkways out of the barn. And it's just when they're on those walkways that some cows decide they have to answer nature's call. It isn't always possible to get them out in time.

I now find the job I can do as well as any man: I sweep the walkways.

An important attraction at the annual Mitchell fall fair is the Crystal Palace. It is filled with pies, fancy cookies, cakes, quilts, pillows, paintings, flowers, fruits, vegetables, and hobby craft, most of it produced by the ladies. Norman and I go through it fairly quickly. Out in the broiling sun and Saturday afternoon crowd again, we meet Norman McCully who is about Norman Coulchard's age. The two discuss the pity of it that they're only going to show the horses tonight and that young folks aren't so interested any more in heavy horses. McCully says he used to do a lot of judging at fairs but now he's getting on and he's a "has-been." Norman likes the expression, and every time he meets a friend this afternoon he tells him he, Norman, is a "has-been," too.

There are cattle on show and brightly coloured farm machines, but what strikes Norman's fancy most is a tiny, noisy steam engine. It is connected to a circular saw and two sweating men demonstrate with old logs. Norman watches in the sun and sawdust while one entire log is slowly squared and cut into planks.

We catch a horse race with three entries ridden by two boys and a girl in their early teens. When they are mounted the track loudspeaker says the girl gets a 100-yard start.

"Why?" the biggest boy wants to know.

"Because she's a girl," says the loudspeaker.

"But it's the horse that's running!" he yells.

The girl comes in last.

I buy Norman a soft drink and he carries the empty cup for an hour until he finds a garbage can.

There's a stand where you can throw balls and, if the bull's-eye is hit, a girl sitting about two yards above it plunges into a tank full of water. We wait for two falls. Norman tells me he is not happy with the attendance at the fair; it used to be much more crowded.

"People are seeing too much these days," he says. "When I was younger, to get out like this was a real treat."

On the way home he is quiet. Then he says suddenly:

"Fairs just aren't what they used to be, but neither am I—so what's the difference?"

———◆◆◆———

Once a year, a group of friends Norman goes deer hunting with organize a party to which they bring their wives. It's tonight and I'm asked along.

In a tree-sheltered spot in a field far from the road, a long table is piled with corn, salads, cold meats, fried chicken, pickles, buns, and pies. A smaller table serves as bar. There are about 50 people, and they've all known each other since school days. Most of them are farmers. In the dark after supper, they show slides of hunting trips in earlier years; then Roy Collie, who is with the Veterans Land Act in Stratford creates clever shadows with his fingers on the lit-up screen and closes with a series of marvellously accurate farm animal sounds! We build a huge fire and sit around singing "Take Me Out to the Ball Game," "Roll Out the Barrel," and more.

I am on my own most of the evening. Nobody is really sure who I am but I'm welcome just the same. Around midnight Norman and I meet at the nearly depleted bar.

"How art thou?" he shouts.

I'm introduced to the group around him as Ernest Hellyer and he says he can't understand why I picked his farm to stay on, and they laugh and say they can't either.

Jeanne drives on the way home.

<hr/>

In our Sunday clothes, we're all sitting in a row in St Andrew's Presbyterian Church in Stratford. The heat doesn't seem to have kept many people away. Norman is an elder here and Jeanne is involved in an executive capacity on a variety of committees.

Sometime during the service, Reverend James Ferguson suggests that, if we're sitting next to a stranger, we should right now take a few moments and get acquainted. Then he launches into his sermon, "The Gospel of Labour." It is sprinkled with quotes from C. Wright Mills and Milton and others.

Later, during the social hour, Ferguson asks Norman and his sons about the new combine bought three weeks ago. He listens like a man who knows about combines.

<hr/>

Evening chores are done but Sunday isn't over yet. We all get dressed up again and drive two miles to watch Gordon and Winston play baseball.

"City people," says Winston, "can crawl in a corner and do nothing on weekends. Not us—we got to be busy."

Most of the players are in their 30s. During one game, I note that both the pitcher and the catcher are in their late 50s. Both are feared batters as well.

There must be at least 150 people here. The players have all brought their families to cheer for them. Jeanne is up with the women on the bleachers. Norman has found a couple of cronies to talk to. I am tired and watch without much interest. After church, we had gone home and pitched horseshoes till dinner. Then drove 30 miles to Woodstock to attend an open house of Western Ontario Breeders Incorporated. We looked at the bulls, were served two gratis portions of ice cream and all the chocolate milk we could drink. Then supper. Then chores. And now baseball. I want to go to bed.

———— ◦••◦ ————

I ask Norman after chores Monday night if he would like to go for a short walk through his land with me.

The crickets are at it and so are the other insects. The sun is going down, a flaming orange ball. Norman looks at it. "First of September today—summer's gone," he says. "Sometimes I get to thinking, you know, and it's really hard for me to think that I'm this old...."

Larry and Alex are walking with us. We go along the creek until we get to the big willow.

"Usually there are lots of frogs around here," says Larry, "and you can hear them go 'boomp, boomp, boomp.'"

He catches a little green one to show me. It leaps away when he opens his hand and Norman asks him to pick it up and bring it back to the creek's edge where he found it.

I ask if willows often get that big and Norman answers:

"If you let them grow long enough, they will."

The milk cows are gathered under the tree. Some stand in pairs one behind the other so the tail of the one in front keeps the flies off the face of the one behind. Alex cups his hands to his mouth and gives out like an owl. The cows turn to stare at him.

I ask Norman if he ever feels like staying in bed in the morning.

"Well, when morning comes, you know," he says, "and that alarm clock goes off, I do kinda lie there sometimes for a few minutes. But you can only stay for so long, and then you've got to pull yourself together and just, well, just get up. So I get right up and keep going."

I ask him how be feels about owning this land.

"Well, it comes kinda natural like. There's a kinda nice feeling, you know, just for a fella to think he has this land, you know, and he's running it, operating it....It's a nice feeling all right. When you're around it all the time, you kinda forget about it a little bit, but just let me go downtown to Toronto, down to my sister's there, and into that traffic jam, and that rushing, well, when I get home here, why I just *relax* and I'm just as satisfied as a cow laying down chewing her cud."

The Drift to the Cities

People like the Coulchards and their way of life and work are growing increasingly scarce in Canada. In 1901, we had a population of about five million, and 62 percent of the people lived in rural areas; in 1930, it was down to 46 percent, and in 1966, when there were some 20 million people, to 28 percent. Attractive wages and less responsibility in urban areas have pulled young people off the farm, and increasing farm costs, heavier investment, and the inevitable trend toward larger farms and greater specialization are pushing them off. In 1980, when we are expected to have a population of 26 million, the Canadian department of agriculture foresees that just 19 percent of the people will be living in rural areas and that only six percent will be actual farm residents.

Chapter 2

Few and Free

The horse could at least have looked at me. I walked especially slowly so as not to startle him, and said, "Hi horse," but he went on nibbling the lawn. A small lawn in front of a small house on a street in Richmond, BC [1973]. As the windows of the house held the summer sun, so the horse held the path to the front door. I had never seen a horse loose on a city lawn before. I wished he'd get out of the way. I wished he'd at least show he knew I was there. Then the door opened and a smiling blonde woman said:

"Hello!"

And to the horse:

"Move, Lucky, please?"

Sure, the horse raised his head then. He looked at the woman a long moment, took two steps, and went back to trimming the grass.

"He's 40," said Norma Bearcroft. "That's 120 years in human life!"

Lucky didn't look it, and Norma said he also still had all his teeth.

The knocker on the door was the brass head of a horse. And inside, the whole house through, it was a wonderland of horse things. Horses on curtains, pillows, tablecloths, and trays. Horse ash trays, plates, figurines, and clocks. Paintings of horses, photos, pennants, and about 100 books. And all the animals were wild, with manes flying and legs frozen in an eternal gallop.

Norma had more to say about Lucky. In fact, a great deal more to say about horses, particularly wild ones. A small, fiery woman, she glowed as the words rushed. It was her absolute favourite subject. It was hard to stop her, and that was just fine.

Lots of people detest cats, abhor fish, and resent dogs, but who in the world doesn't like horses? Most of us live pressed and fettered in cities and towns. Watch our faces in the street when a horse passes....Then allow yourself a flash vision of a band of wild ones running the hills: it's got to make you smile. They are free. Not very useful maybe, not always as handsome as in Disney films, but free. It's a state of being. And there aren't many of them left.

We only hear of them occasionally, and then it's always bad news. Some fools have shot them up because they're a "nuisance," or for pet food, or for the hell of it. The good news is, I gather, that it doesn't happen much any more: real slaughters as they had up until a half a dozen years ago are a thing of the past. Governments have changed laws and people have changed attitudes. Norma Bearcroft has had a lot to do with that.

Norma is the truest, most loving friend wild horses have in Canada. A court stenographer, she works full time to support herself, Lucky, two Spanish mustangs, a Mexican burro, and five cats. But a vast portion of her time and energy—she has almost no social life—is spent fighting for wild horses. Eight years ago, in 1965, sickened by the continual killing of them, she founded The Canadian Wild Horse Society. She's the secretary-treasurer. This non-profit, charitable organization is dedicated to "the protection and preservation of wild horses and fighting cruelty to all equines." Its policy is simple: leave them alone. The society has won some battles. In 1966, the BC government was pressured into stopping bounties, and two years later discontinued slaughter permits. In Alberta, the minister of lands and forests announced, "Wild horses will be rounded up only when they create severe ecological or biological damage."

Norma works at least two hours a day for the horses. She edits the society's quarterly, *Cayuse Conserver*, corresponds with hundreds of guides, outfitters, and others who know wild horses, and has recently organized a $6,000 research project to determine precisely what the animals eat. She's written several books on horses and compiled five others. One of her books, *Wild Horses of Canada*, is out of print but she plans to reissue it and include a batch of new material. She spends most of her vacations searching for and observing the stallions and their bands of mares.

Lucky, I learned, was an ex-wild horse from the Cariboo and probably the oldest in BC. Part of his tongue is missing because he was quick-broken with a barbed-wire bit. He eats the same food as Norma's other horses, and the vet says he doesn't want to put him to sleep because he seems to be enjoying life so much. Strangers, as noted earlier, don't bother Lucky: he ignores them; same with cameras. But one thing that scares him is lightning. When a storm breaks, Norma rushes out and horse-sits.

When Lucky was a youngster, there were perhaps 100,000 wild horses in Canada. Today, Norma figures, there may be 1,000 in BC, another 2,000 in Alberta, some uncounted bands in Saskatchewan, and a few hundred on Sable Island in the Atlantic Ocean. Four thousand at most. They'll survive, she thinks, if enough people want them to. Some experts involved with preserving wildlife say they see the faint beginning in this country of a different attitude toward killing wild things for the sport or thrill of it. They say the young, particularly, don't see it as such he-man action any more. It's one thing, for instance, to blast a bullet into an animal from 100 yards, another to catch a sharp close-up of it with a camera.

"Where," I asked Norma, "can I find some wild horses?" She got a map and pointed to where one guide reported seeing 20 and somewhere else another said he had spotted 40, and then way up in Dawson Creek, 380 miles northwest of Edmonton, Frank Cooke claimed 100 ran on his land.

———◆━◆◆━◆———

Frank Cooke, 46, six-foot-one, looked wrong in Dawson Creek, out of place. In the wilderness, 100 miles from the nearest road, he looked right. He's lived there all his life and carved a hunting empire from it. Ten years ago he was broke with seven children to feed. Now he and his three sons run the biggest guiding-outfitting operation in northern BC. This fall they'll handle 75 customers, mostly rich Americans. Many of them will be after stone sheep. The hunters stay 15 days for a flat $3,000. Cooke & Sons are booked through to 1975.

"But," said Cooke, "I think hunting'll phase out in ten years at most. People'll come to take pictures, go fishing, boating. More the dude ranch kind of thing. You can't kill game forever, you know."

His land—where he has exclusive hunting rights—runs some 200 miles south from the Yukon Territory border, 150 miles at its widest. Headquarters are in the Kechika Valley on Scoop Lake, about 100 miles west of Fort Nelson.

There was a delay of several days in Dawson Creek waiting for the weather "to quit socking up over the mountains." When it did, one of the sons, Terry, 22, piloted the Cessna 185. There wasn't much conversation. The land below was too awesome. Peace River country, and then suddenly row upon row of the mighty snow peaks. In between, swirling winds tried to grab us. The sun was king that day and vision was unlimited.

Father and son had flown the route hundreds of times in all seasons. But over the engine's drone one might yell to the other, "Goddamn, this is pretty country!" And minutes later, the other, pointing to some narrow valley deep in shadow, might shout, "Damn beautiful, I'd say!"

Once Cooke called out: "When I get on one of them peaks in August, I'll just sit down and tell the world to go to hell!"

We flew back and forth over the valley a bit before landing, trying to spot horses. There were lots of moose, maybe 25 in ten minutes. Then, less than five miles from the airstrip—horses.

"Wild, for sure!" yelled Terry, swooping in.

Six. Long-maned, long-tailed, one of them clean white, up to their knees in a tiny lake eating the green goose-grass just beneath the water's surface. They looked incredibly vulnerable as the plane bore down on them. Their heads shot up and instantly they charged for shore and cover—so fast!—the white one the last to dive beneath the trees. Six wild horses. It was a bit of a moment.

In the bunkhouse drinking coffee, Cooke said: "The thing that saves horses in this valley is the wind. It blows the snow off the ground so they can get at the grass. But if you hit a real bad winter, a lot of 'em die. The ones you saw probably came from the first horses brought up here in '38."

One of his corrals held three two-year-olds. Wild ones, caught a few days earlier by another son, Frankie. His father said Frankie had a gift for handling horses.

"He's kind and quiet and he's got patience. Patience makes the horseman."

The three hadn't been hard to capture. They had mixed with some tame horses in the bush and wandered back with them. Slowly, a bit sadly, they moved around the corral getting used to the saddles on their backs. Already the horses didn't shy away from Frankie or his father. When fall came, they would go to work as riding or pack horses, said Cooke, and each would be worth about $350.

"You've got to catch wild horses young," he said. "Old ones'll worry themselves to death. They won't eat. They're like some men when you put 'em in jail.

"I've got 15 wild colts right now. If we left here and didn't come back for a bunch of years, this whole valley would be full of mustangs!"

What a thought!

Cooke pointed north. "I know of one strawberry roan and an old black 30 miles up there...."

His hand swung east. "Across the river there, a dapple grey and a black. Once in a while you see 'em on a side of a hill....I leave 'em be."

Terry took me up again and for more than an hour we dipped into valleys and circled mountains looking for more wild horses. We saw about 30. Most dashed out of sight when we came in low. The bush hid them totally. But one band of five just watched as we roared in once, and didn't move as we swung about for a second look.

Cooke was in a fit when we got back. One of his boats carrying two outboard motors had broken loose from its mooring and floated down river. A possible loss of $5,000. Everybody was ordered to go looking for it. That included Frankie. We had planned that Frankie would take me on horseback to some hills where I might get a peek at wild ones fairly close up. I was sorry it was not to be.

The boat was safely retrieved. But by then it was late afternoon and the plane was due back in Dawson Creek that night.

The return flight was much the same as coming in. Not a lot was said. Now and then one of us would point to a moose below or the white foam from a beaver dam. Cooke dozed off in the back seat. Terry concentrated on flying. It was getting rougher, clouds were forming, occasionally rain lashed the aircraft. We were skimming the colossal peaks again. And then a sudden thought struck Terry, a wilderness man like his father, one who would not live in any other land.

"It's kind of nice to know," he shouted, "that there are those horses running around....That they're not all caught!"

And that's all he said until he made contact with the control tower.

Chapter 3

Where They Work
Only Two Months a Year

They gossip a lot on Entry Island—and why not? In winter, especially, life there needs all the spice it can get. A bleak, forlorn place, it hasn't really got much excuse to harbour life. Lashed by wind and snow, it sticks out through the jagged ice floes of the Gulf of St Lawrence, isolated even from its fellow Magdalen Islands in Quebec.

God only knows why humans settled there. But they did—fishermen. And they built small wooden houses that face west toward the archipelago's southeasterly "hook," about five miles across the water. In winter they stoked their homes sweat-hot and gossiped. And their descendants gossip. They work only about two months a year. You can't fish in winter, you see, and on Entry there isn't much else to do. Not for a visitor either.

Now, "gossip" here also means arguing, storytelling, opinionating, reminiscing, and so on. There's a lot less of that than in the old days—every home on Entry has television. And this past winter there was still less—they had a job of work to do.

That job was one reason for my visit. The other: who ever heard of Entry Island?

In January, 1973, the island received a $102,404 Local Initiative Program (LIP) grant from Ottawa. It created 73 jobs for the 100-person labour force of the 255 population. A clean-up scheme: dismantle ruins of houses, clear beaches of refuse, drag away abandoned cars, build a single large tackle and bait shed from the lumber of many small, old ones, tidy up and fence in the island's first cemetery, dig one big watering hole for the cattle, and install cupboards, tables, running water, and toilets in the community hall.

It might provide jobs right through to the end of April, nearly the start of fishing season. Pay—$90 per week on the average—came to twice what people could get from unemployment insurance. The plan was proposed and managed by two islanders, Stuart and Garry Josey, aged 22 and 21.

And so one miserable February morning, I was on the back of Stuart's snowmobile racing along nine twisting miles of the ice bridge between Amherst Island and Entry. Some people like snowmobiles and some people don't like the noisy, stinking, dangerous things. Stuart had had an accident the week before. His freckled face was still covered with blood-encrusted stitches; the wind on them must have hurt. A slim, intense man, he didn't say much. Once he yelled over his shoulder, "Snowmobiles have cut winter in half!"

The trail across the contorted ice was marked or "bushed" with branches stuck in the snow. In a storm few would have been visible. Islanders, I was later told, often made the trip at night, drunk. Sometimes we seemed to be doubling back, circumventing cracks or dark patches that mean thin ice or no ice at all. Four minutes in that water and you're dead. We whined and slipped and jumped for more than an hour. In the old days, the islanders used horses. Coming back, foxes would track the smell of the horses and that's how some came to live on Entry. Foxes don't do that with snowmobiles.

Entry is two miles at its longest and seven miles around. The western half, where people live, forms a gentle slope. Then it turns rugged and hilly with the highest peak 680 feet above sea level. In summer, the island's cliffs are said to be lavishly tinted with a mixture of brown sandstone, ochre, and grey gypsum. In winter, the island looked just like another, if very big, hunk of ice. As we got closer, scattered black dots slowly turned into houses. Nothing moved. Then a youngster rode out of a shack bareback on a horse. He stopped and watched us rocket ashore.

There are 22 horses on the island, one saddle, 43 snowmobiles, and 21 fishing boats. Entry has a Red Cross clinic, a lighthouse, a school, a post office, and a church. It doesn't have one advertising sign. Everybody knows where the four small food stores are, and what's doing at the hall. Of the island's 3,200 acres, 312 are in pasture. Nearly every family keeps a few cattle, sheep, chickens, and pigs. Everybody grows their own winter's supply of potatoes. The average income is between $3,000 and $3,600, yet only two people keep a vegetable garden. Every time I asked about this they said they used to in the old days but not anymore. Why not? Well...they didn't.

Hot lunch was waiting at the Josey home—mashed potatoes, carrots, boiled beef. Josey is one of the 13 main surnames on Entry. The others are Aitkins, McLean, Chesnell, Clark, Quinn, Dickson, Patton, Cassidy, Collins, Goodwin, Morrison, and Welsh. One of the Welsh girls, Lena, is Stompin' Tom Connors' lady friend. Everybody remembered when Tom visited Entry.

All those families are related. Blue eyes, freckles, and blond or carrot-coloured hair are extraordinarily common: also, apparently, too many people on that little island suffer from diabetes, poor eyesight, deafness, etc. The fact that there's considerable malnutrition doesn't help either—due to dietary ignorance, not lack of money; many families eat four full meals a day. And a lot of people's teeth looked in poor condition; I saw teenagers with no teeth at all.

The Joseys were fine hosts. Ancil, 55, runs one of the four stores and also has the island's beer outlet. At the start of the Second World War, virtually every able-bodied man volunteered. Fourteen landed in the Royal Rifles. They went to Hong Kong, were captured by the Japanese, and spent the next three years and eight months in prison. Ancil is one of the six who came back.

Olive Josey, an ample, energetic woman, is the mother of six, of whom the youngest is 11. Every day she tramps four miles to teach at the school. Two years ago she decided to get her teacher's degree and attended university full time in Charlottetown. She serves on the island's council and plans to run for mayor at the next election.

The one I got to know best in the family was the LIP project's other manager, Garry. Blond, soft-spoken, and very serious about his job, he did most of the showing around. He had to borrow Stuart's snowmobile; he hasn't got one because he's saving up for a bulldozer. It was he, though, who said: "It was an entirely different island until the machines came....Cars and trucks in summer. Snowmobiles in winter."

We set out to inspect the project. We watched cursing fishermen slowly pull an old car across the white hills. It was blowing hard, and leaning single-file on the rope they looked like Siberian convicts. Others were hacking a ditch in the frozen earth so water could be piped to the community hall. We travelled to the old cemetery (the new one is behind the church). It was a windless spot, ringed by broken, weathered fencing where just two headstones poked through the snow. Garry showed the bare flat places where abandoned houses had already been pulled down. In the community hall, cupboards and tables were nearly done and work was starting on the toilets. The islanders are good at carpentry. All the homes, old as well as new, are self-built.

There was perhaps most enthusiasm for working in the hall. Out of the weather, for one thing. But also because it's the one place where everybody gets together. Church services, nowadays, are at best sporadic. Apparently Entry isn't important enough to have a regular minister. I was told that in the old days the church was always full. Nor does anyone seem to worry much about transportation and postal services for Entry in winter. Three or more weeks will go by without mail. As the mayor told me, "We had better services in the '20s than now." In the very old days, of course, they would simply push a sealed mackerel barrel off Amherst and hope it would drift over with the tide. It did sometimes, but might also land in Cape Breton or PEI. And, because of lack of transportation, Red Cross nurse Ann Robertson had recently to call too often on the Search and Rescue Service for hospital emergencies.

So getting the hall fixed is important. Once a week, weather permitting, there's Bingo; once a month, a dance with a liquor licence which pulls in as many as 50 couples.

Garry said of the project: "It used to be guys lay in bed till 11 or 12. Nothing to do. Now they've got something to look forward to. People are realizing we have a beautiful community. It isn't just the money. It's pride."

Though the responsibility is theirs, neither Garry nor Stuart makes more than the others.

"It's not a bad feeling," said Garry, "to know you've helped people. Not to make a profit, but just to help."

Said brother Stuart: "I believe everybody will be free of debt by the end of the project. That's my hope, anyway, and the reason we put in for it."

A few islanders were skeptical. They said the extra money was going on booze and new snowmobiles. But most of those asked agreed with Stuart.

Harold Dickson, 23, six-foot-three, married with one child, was foreman on the project. His winter's fuel had cost $325, food $500. That was all paid off. "I'm working for my own now," he said. "Come spring, we're going to get a bathroom and maybe a cheap half-ton truck."

That took care of '73. During the lobstering (May 9–July 10) he would fish with 300 traps. Afterwards there might be a little scallop, mackerel, and cod fishing. If he did well, he could make $4,500, or about $1,000 after expenses. What about the '74 winter then?

"Well," smiled the big man, "being a fisherman is being a gambler....And remember, we all own our homes. On the mainland my house might have cost $20,000. But here it's very little—no labour to pay."

Still, it seemed like quite a struggle. Would he take off if a lot of money suddenly came his way?

Harold didn't give a yes or a no. "Fishing...," he said, "it's something you do yourself. You're your own man."

Garry and I accompanied Jim McLean, one of his mother's brothers, and a Labrador retriever named Jet on a fruitless, early morning duck hunt. We walked a mile onto the sea to a wide break showing black water. Jim threw pieces of ice in the water for Jet to go after so I could see what a good retriever he was. Jet whined and yelped and ran around but decided it was silly to jump in just for ice.

Jim recalled that once on a hunt he had fallen in himself. "That's when you think about God," he said. "Never think about Him till you need Him, I guess."

Jim and Garry told about Jet's behaviour many times afterwards. A tiny incident, it was never made out to more than that, just often repeated, always listened to with interest and, no doubt, remembered.

Garry also told it to Dorothy Quinn, and she would remember it forever. Mrs Quinn, 79, has the undisputed best memory on Entry. Somebody should sit her down with a tape recorder. A birthday, a death, a name, the weather in early June, 1947—Mrs Quinn remembers. She lives in the oldest house on the island with her bachelor son, Ivan. From her front window she looks down on most of the other homes.

She didn't much enjoy being interviewed; she liked asking questions. But still she talked a little: "People aren't the same....Used to be the island was like one. We were happy...all the women washing together at Wash Pond. We didn't drink as much then either!"

Her grey eyes looked out the window. Not a tree in sight. There are still patches of dwarf spruce on Entry, but not many. "Used to be forest right to the beach," she said. "You could hear the little birds singing in the summertime."

She said it was Norman Goodwin's 81st birthday that day, that there were precisely 235 persons on Entry, with 20 more "away" at school, and she told the story of the horse.

It happened on March 7, 1923, the year she got married, that a man from Grosse Île (another Magdalen island, *50 miles north*) exchanged horses with the father of Russell McLean, Entry's current mayor, and that man then rode his new horse, Farmer, across the ice all the way to Grosse Île. The following July, Farmer disappeared...to rise up out of the sea and trot up Entry's beach, later that same month. He made straight for his former master's home, who never let him go again.

Mrs Quinn told the story sitting by the stove in slippers. On a shelf by her head a clock ticked. The last thing she said was: "The Rangers are going to take it this year."

Mayor McLean, 44, sat rocking in the kitchen of his small, neat bachelor home. He said, yes, the project was a marvelous thing for his community. He himself worked on it, too. He said there was no policeman on Entry and there really was no crime. There was no fisheries department official either, and nobody poached. On the wall above his chair, hung a small wooden sign that said:

"Work…the Curse of the Drinking Class." He said he had bought it in PEI. McLean, a cousin of Olive Josey, said he had, in his time, worked as far west as Edmonton.

"But I don't like the mainland much," he said. "Too noisy."

Like the others on the island, McLean liked to let you see old things. He held out a tiny white clay pipe with an elephant and palm trees carved on the head. His grandmother used to smoke it.

So Garry showed me his island, and seemed to enjoy it—"We know we're not known."

The visits left some impressions. There probably still is a good deal of superstition. (The best way to avoid infection when you step on a rusty nail is simply to burn the nail.) There's obvious respect for the old from the young, and vice versa. (The Josey brothers, supervising many who are their senior, are an example.) There's little respect for one another's privacy. Every home has a phone with about seven phones to a line. Everybody knows that everybody else listens in. (Except perhaps, I was told, when the soap opera "Guiding Light" is on because every islander watches that.) The most lasting impression, though, has to be that they are proud, self-contained, patient, hospitable people.

The last visit was with Lindbergh Patton. Said to be Entry's best fisherman, he is, at 43, also the father of the largest family—12, four married with eight of their own. Patton hasn't a grey hair on his head. He, too, expected, for once, to be debt-free by the end of winter. If this was a good year, said Patton, there might be a few dollars left over. He might then visit two of his married daughters in Montreal. It would be his third time off Entry.

Olive Josey had hinted there might be a party. Sure enough, the night before I was to leave, snowmobile-suited men and women started crowding into the kitchen. One brought a guitar, another a fiddle, a third a three-inch mouth organ, which she played holding a small glass at the end. One bare, very strong light glared from the ceiling. After they carried out the dining table and fridge, everybody sat in straight chairs along the walls, not saying much. They chewed gum, sipped rye, and tapped their feet to "Rubber Dolly," "Maple Sugar," and "The Wreck of the Old '97." Olive was first on the floor, dragging Ancil along. After a couple of rounds, Stuart took over from his father, and pretty soon everybody was going. In thick woollen socks, they circled, bowed, stamped, swung, and sweated. Around 10, a tall, middle-aged man wandered in, blue eyes swimming. He watched the fun for a minute, then slowly and straight as a tree keeled over—out before he hit the floor. The dancers never missed a step.

The Josey sons dispensed liquor and beer and were generous hosts. The kitchen door was left open, but it didn't affect the heat; water streamed from the windows. The dancers accompanied themselves with whoops and howls. Gradually, some grew less sure-footed. But they persevered, as did the musicians, till, oh, I don't know, 2 or 3 AM.

I recall someone shouting: "If you don't have fun now, you won't have it later! Have it now!"

The ride back across the ice bridge next morning was as mad as the one coming in. Some of the drivers had been dancers. Three times they stopped. Unhurriedly, backs against the wind, they rolled smokes and passed around beers.

They weren't crossing to Amherst especially for me. Why then? Well, it was Saturday, no work on the project, something to do, maybe buy a case of beer....

Presumably, were it not for the project, they might be aimlessly riding the ice weekdays as well. The brothers Josey have the beginnings of a scheme for next winter—planting trees, building a skating rink and a playground, cleaning elderly people's homes— and maybe they'll make it work again. But what about the winter after that?

I heard the rumour on the island that one day they might all be moved off and settled where there was more work. Entry would become a park. It might be a solution, but a unique community will have disappeared then.

Father Frédéric Landry is pastor of Amherst. A native of the Magdalens, he's been doing research on the islands for years. He has set up a small museum, published a map of all the shipwrecks in the area, and has just written a book about the islands. The ideal man to talk to about Entry.

"You cannot," said Father Landry, "compare it really with any other community. That island, *Monsieur*, is a mystery."

Chapter 4

"You Spend Your Life on Horses Who Want Nothing More Than to Get You Off"

Store signs squeaked in the raw October wind; less than a dozen cars and pickups were parked on Castor's Main Street. Yet it was Friday afternoon and there was the rodeo that night. An event, you would think, in a town of 1,200, more than 160 miles northeast of Calgary. But even the tavern in the Cosmopolitan Hotel was almost empty. Four bearded Hutterites in black coats sat at one table, a red-faced man wearing a cowboy hat at another. The man tipped back his hat and, so help me, he shouted:

"Siddown, pardner!"

No, people hadn't forgotten about the rodeo. They'd show up soon enough. Drive in from a hundred miles! Hell, this was the last rodeo this season in Canada. Big names coming. Bareback champ Dale Trotter, calf roper Jim Gladstone and...guess who? Kenny Mclean!

"He's good, huh?"

"Lissen," said the red-faced man. "Out east they've got their goddam Jean Béliveau and goddam Bobby Orr. Here we've got our goddam Kenny McLean!"

7:30 PM and already the smells of livestock and french fries hung pretty heavy in Castor's hockey rink. The place had a capacity of

1,200, but more were jamming in. Many wore big hats. I had an appointment with the famous rider. He sat alone on a wooden bench, by the door, legs crossed, smoking, and staring at the ground. He didn't seem aware of the crowd and the noise. He wore the inevitable hat and scuffed boots. No spurs; he wasn't riding till the second night. He rose in one motion, his body like a single muscle. The mouth flashed gold, two bits of it on an upper front, but the dark eyes took deliberate measure. Kenny McLean is a star and talks to a lot of reporters. Sometimes they can be overbearing, and sometimes they can hurt. So he shook hands with reserve. The hands were wide and very clean and set on extraordinarily wide wrists. The one I handled felt like untanned leather.

And then in the lowest, easiest, purest-Texan drawl: "Evening! What say we find us a seat in there?"

McLean was from Vernon, BC, though. Did they drawl in Vernon?

"Don't rightly know...." he drawled.

He seemed to be thinking on it and if, while talking, his face hadn't been very expressive, when he stopped, it revealed nothing. "I spend a lot of time down south," he said. "Maybe I picked it up there."

Just as we had won two seats near the chutes, everybody rose to hear "The Cowboy's Prayer." It signalled the start of the rodeo. Over an ill-adjusted PA system, the emcee boomed:

"And when we make that last inevitable ride to the country up there beyond, where the grass grows lush, green, and stirrup-high, and the water runs cool, clear, and deep, we ask that You as our last Judge will tell us that our entry fees have been paid. Amen!"

Sitting down, Kenny said that he had paid a $20 entry fee for each of his events Saturday night: bronc riding, calf roping, and steer wrestling. I learned later just how unusual this is, entering three events. Of the roughly 600 professional rodeo cowboys in Canada [1973], half a dozen make their full-time living in rodeo and, of the 3,000 in the US, about 75 do. Of those 80-odd, only about a dozen are good enough to compete profitably in two or three events. Apparently, it's a little like Nancy Greene going in for jumping and the downhill and the slalom.

Then the first rider exploded out of a chute on a snorting, twisting wild thing that absolutely didn't want him there. It leapt, kicked, and spun, groaning with the effort. The leather rigging gave off peculiar snarls. On television it had never looked so hard; up close it was fearful. Each time a manned bucking horse charges into an arena he's going to school, learning another trick to pitch people off his back. A good bucker fetches $4,500, and some are still at it at age 20. The horse threw the rider just after the signal. The man's boot stuck in the stirrup and the crowd gasped as he was jerked along, head among flying hoofs, until he made a quick belly flop and the boot slipped free.

"One way to make a dollar!"

"Yeah," allowed McLean.

For him, it comes to about $20,000 a year. There are 540 official rodeos in Canada and the US, and Kenny now gets to an average of 50. In his 16-year career—he is 33 now—he has attended about 1,200 rodeos and ridden some 3,000 broncos, wrestled 2,000 steers and roped 5,000 calves. Falls totalled about 100. He has broken a foot, broken his nose three times, and cracked a number of ribs. He's had muscles torn loose from his ribs, wrists sprained, knees twisted, three teeth knocked out, thumbs forced out of joint, and ears, neck, face, and arms burned by rope. On his back he carries scars of whip-like cuts from when horses reared up in chutes and smashed him against the boards. And every July, for some reason, Kenny pulls the muscles in his groin.

"I've been lucky," he said. "A lot get more broken up than that. I've seen one bull rider stepped on and killed...."

What about fear then? Kenny's eyes stayed glued to the arena as another cowboy burst from a chute.

"If I'd get feared of horses, I'd quit. A horse falling backward in a chute and pinning you is pretty scary, I guess. And I don't ride bulls because they're dangerous. Afraid of 'em, I suppose."

When there was action in the ring, he clearly preferred to watch. "Some think when you've seen one rodeo you've seen them all. But there's always something different, something to learn."

Watching and learning, he believes, has a lot to do with getting to and staying at the top. And it's a habit that he continually reminds himself not to neglect. He knows he can still lose. In 1971, for instance, he drove 800 miles right through the night from Texas to a rodeo in Denver, Colorado, where he might have won

$10,000. He paid $250 in entry fees, contested six times—and didn't make a dime.

So, through much of the calf roping, bull riding, barrel racing, steer wrestling, and the clown act, we sat in silence. One clown broke his hand but kept right on. A horse bucked so hard it broke its own back—something Kenny had never seen before. (The horse had to be killed.) Rider after rider came on and took their chances. The crowd whooped, hollered, and stamped its feet.

Once Kenny said: "I drew a bad horse for tomorrow. There's good and bad, and Chuckwagon is bad. He doesn't buck enough."

And I interrupted once to ask about cowboys and liquor and women and hell-raising. It produced the longest quote in two days:

"It don't mix—riding and drinking. Not if you're going to rodeo, man! You've got to be an athlete. That's what we are—*athletes*.

"There's always women. Camp followers, come for the good times. They're available if you want them...and I think they always will be.

"Cowboys can raise hell like anybody. But they're spotted because they wear hats. If they didn't wear hats, who would know? If hockey players went out and had their fun in uniform—well, there'd be a lot of publicity about them. Nowadays, cowboys aren't any more rough than anybody. All those rodeo movies lately are full of phony parts. Cowboys just don't act like that anymore."

After the rodeo there was a dance. Kenny brought his vivacious, dark-eyed wife Joyce. On this trip their three-year-old son Guy had been left with his grandparents in Vernon.

The place was packed and the sound system turned to blast, so we stayed only briefly. But the next morning a young cowboy from Saskatoon said there had been a gigantic fight around 2. Some pipeliners had come in, he said, slapped $500 on the bar, and yelled, "Free booze for ten minutes!" Things got out of hand after that. A scuffle turned mean and apparently most people joined in.

"It was," said the young cowboy, "an ocean of fighters!"

He looked at me. "I knew you were in town," he said, "and with the press and all. So I got up on a chair to see better....And you better report there wasn't one of us cowboys fighting!"

Castor's cafes were full of rodeo friends, so Kenny and I drove 38 miles west to Stettler for a quiet breakfast and talk. The latter wasn't so easy.

Kenny is on the road about 11 months of the year. Rarely more than two weeks in one place, often just a day, he drives from rodeo to rodeo over a vast part of this continent. Home, then, is a 14-foot trailer, complete with shower, toilet, and TV. Since they were married six years ago, Joyce has travelled with him everywhere, as has Guy since he was six months old. Self-sufficient, mobile, rootless, it is a gypsy life, running on the whim, will, and luck of the man in the driver's seat. Kenny has no agent or manager; his schedule is his own. Income depends on where and how frequently and how well he competes—there are no guarantees of any kind. Half the money earned, incidentally, goes to travel expenses. So far he hasn't been badly hurt, which, in part, he admitted, is due to luck. His profession can't be very popular with insurance companies. Even the $25,000 life policy he holds with the Canadian Rodeo Cowboys' Association costs $500 a year.

If whim and luck have worked well for him, it's the will, you feel, that's really done it. For a long time he seems to have known what he wanted, and single-mindedly he's worked to achieve and then maintain it. He gives the impression he knows who he is. The answer is in rodeo.

To do well at it requires skill, know-how, a special instinct, and physical fitness. The maintenance and improvement of those seemed to be Kenny's preoccupation—not one, I guessed, that called for much talking. And Kenny himself said that he found talking difficult, especially in public. And that's what he was asked to do, in a way, over breakfast in Stettler. He was willing and patient, but also, a little, like the proverbial coiled spring. Questions got longer and answers shorter.

Eight sentences asking, "How do you stay in shape?" would get a brief and disconcertingly complete reply like this: "I try to do things the hard way. I'll jump over a gate instead of walking through it."

There was rarely any elaboration. Joyce later attested to this. "If I happen to miss a contest," she said, "I'll ask him, 'How did it go?' And he'll say, 'Fine,' and that's all. A while later, there's the trophy on the fridge. "Not many people know him, really. He keeps everything to himself."

But bits and pieces did come out. He told me about his saddle, for instance. While he's won 33 of them, he had, of course, his own that he always competed on. He'd had it since 1959 and trusted it. Last spring in Seattle it was stolen. Since then he often rode on borrowed saddles.

"A lot of men," said Kenny, "get a mental block when they lose their saddles. The confidence goes. I set out to prove different— that I could ride as well on a borrowed saddle."

Many people fear there's cruelty to animals in rodeos. Kenny said this may have been so in the past, but wasn't any more. Among its bylaws, his association has a list of 15 strict and specific ones in this regard as well as the ruling that a "contestant will be disqualified for any mistreatment of livestock." (At Castor, there was always an SPCA man on duty at the chutes.) He added that a lot of bucking horses, useless for any other work, would end up as glue or dog food much sooner if it weren't for rodeos.

And Kenny gave me this incredible description of bronco riding: "If you're in time with the horse, your feet go forward when he kicks, and when he goes up, they go back. It's like sitting in a rocking chair."

Obviously Kenny relished rodeo life, but there had to be some aspects he didn't like. Could he list them for me? "All the driving," said Kenny.

As a performer he must have had his share of embarrassing moments in public. Had he, for instance, ever split his pants? No. But once at a small show in southern Alberta he had roped his calf, leapt off his horse, jerked the calf off its feet, thrown it on its side, was ready to whip his "pegging" string around its legs when he realized he'd forgotten the string.

The audience howled, of course, but that didn't bother him. "I never think of them in the stands," Kenny said. "I try to please myself. If I fall or miss out there, it's not them, it's me. And if I do good, I know it, too."

Kenny was raised on his father's ranch at Okanagan Falls, ten miles south of Penticton, BC. His paternal grandfather was a Scot; most of his other ancestors were Indian. Had this background affected his rodeo life? "I'm not an Indian or a white man. I'm just myself," said Kenny.

Some people, I suggested, might consider riding horses that don't want you to a silly way to make a living. Why was he a rodeo man?

"I've never really thought about it," said Kenny. "Rodeo is a job for me. I broke a lot of colts as a youngster, and then I set myself goals: national champ, world champ....You're conquering, I guess. It's a challenge. There are horses bucking now that a lot of people can't ride. If I can ride them, well, then I feel real good."

Kenny said he'd be quite happy if his son Guy—who already rides and ropes their Australian collie—went into rodeo.

He saw himself riding broncos another three years; roping and bulldogging quite a few more. Meanwhile, he also wanted to get into business, training horses for both ranching and rodeos. So rodeos were here to stay then?

"Definitely. I'd just like to see them go east, go national."

We returned to Castor and Kenny went to sleep. After performing that night, he planned to drive the 700-odd miles back to Vernon, before, a day or so later, setting off for San Francisco. But Joyce was free.

"He's quiet and shy and good," she said of her husband. "And like the Pied Piper with children. Teaching roping to Guy or strange kids at a rodeo—he's like a cat with kittens.

"And there's another way he's a cat. When he's thrown, he always lands on his feet. He's not thrown often, mind you. He's more capable on a bucking horse than I am in high heels on flat ground. We were married three years before I saw him thrown for the first time—and, sure, he landed on his feet. I swear he's related to the cat family!"

Joyce and I watched the second night's rodeo from the stands. Kenny stayed down by the chutes. When among other riders, he seemed to listen mostly. Then he'd wander away to practise a little roping, or help somebody saddle up, or talk to men just about to slam out of the chute.

"He's giving tips," said Joyce. "And a few need encouragement. But he never does any 'ride 'em' yelling, he's too busy studying that animal."

But most of the time Kenny seemed to be sitting alone on a gate, smoking, eyes hidden by his hat.

If anything, the crowd was happier and louder than on Friday night, maybe an after-effect of the big fight. The floor trembled under thundering feet. And the people roared with pleasure when, well after intermission, the emcee finally announced "that great cowboy" Kenny McLean on Chuckwagon.

Ten seconds. How to distinguish bad from good from superb? Chuckwagon seemed to be bucking plenty. Kenny was sitting in his damn rocking chair; no strain at all. It looked as easy as on television. For one second of those ten, man and horse seemed to become one. And, after the signal, a fluid slide down and a neat feet-landing. Superb, I decided.

So did the judges. Another trophy for McLean (and $198). The lady who handed it to him got a flash of gold, the yelling stands not a glance.

Joyce said: "His left foot hung in the neck too long!"

Within minutes "that great cowboy" was on again. Calf roping. Loud applause.

A blur of a running calf pursued by a horseman and a rope striking like a snake. Briefly, man and calf struggled and then the animal was lying on its side, rear legs tied to a front one, and the man was walking back to his horse. An effortless thing—10.8 seconds. Half the hockey rink was on its feet. Another trophy (plus $201.96) said the judges; the lady got another hint of gold.

And Joyce said: "He fumbled his tie. It could've been 9.8."

The All-Around trophy was now Kenny's also, and would be presented later. There remained steer wrestling and a possible fourth trophy. The idea is for the wrestler, while on his horse, to catch the steer by its horns as it races out of the chute. Then he has to stop and twist it down until it's lying flat on its side, its feet and head straight.

This is what I think I saw: the steer came flying out and Kenny was instantly beside it, leaning far, far over, pretty well out of his saddle, reaching for the horns...and the steer stopped dead. I had watched it happen twice before, and skill and strength were of no use then to those riders. As they grabbed thin air, their momentum had catapulted them over the horns and smacked them to the ground.

Kenny, too, went diving straight forward, heading for a grace-less fall. Then, in mid-air, he seemed to slow down, braking. He raised his head, lowered his legs, shifted his weight, steered that body, flew it a little, and at precisely his own speed hit the ground on ready toes. He ran a few steps to regain balance, turned, and made for the chutes. Crowd response was three or four seconds slow. It let out a disappointed "Ahhhhhhhh!" No fourth trophy for McLean.

But Joyce said: "See what I told you. Kenny the cat!"

McLean's Record

This, considerably abbreviated, is Kenny McLean's record: he entered his first rodeo at 17. Six years later, in 1962, he won the World Championship in bronco riding. He won the Canadian All-Around Championship in 1967, 1968, 1969, and again in 1972. In Canada, he holds the record for total money won, most money won in a single year, and most money won in a single event in one year.

"Somebody From a Big Family Knows Better How to Live Together"

"Yes, I'd have a big family again if I were starting out," said Jim Shanahan, father of nine. "I was always sure I'd be able to support them. Yet...ten years ago, it was still considered a good thing to have a lot of children. There was no stigma. Now, sometimes, I sense veiled suggestions....In five years it may be thought a bad thing."

It was a cold Saturday morning in January [1972]. The Shanahans were breakfasting leisurely, some still in pyjamas and housecoats. The sun poured through the windows of their oldish, yellow two-storey house on a tree-lined country road in Rosemere, a suburb of Montreal. It's a house you regret leaving. It's safe inside.

I went to see them because big families are growing scarce in Canada and, therefore, something basic to the life of this country is disappearing. I wanted to get an idea of what it's like to live in one. I was also invited....

Brenda Shanahan, age 13, had written out of the blue:

Dear Weekend Magazine,
I have a suggestion for an article. How about one about the typical large family, like mine! We've got eleven people, two cats, and a white mouse, and are doing very nicely. Few people from average families (which are supposed to have 2–3 children) know

about the happiness (?) of a live-in gang. I'm the third child and oldest girl in my family, and I've three brothers and five sisters, so naturally I suggest my family.

Anyways,

Brenda Shanahan

P.S. My parents know. I've told them

P.S. This is not a crank letter.

Brenda was right; people probably *would* like to read about a "typical" large family. But she was wrong to describe hers as typical. They are not. What family is when you get to know them? But if the Shanahans were typical…this would be a *different* country!

All were present and, fairly solemnly, there were introductions with handshaking and briefly locking eyes—parents Jim and Joyce, Stephen, 16, Richard, 15, Brenda the writer, the twins Frances and Mary, 12, Ruth, 11, Russell, nine, Jackie, eight, and Sheila, who smiled but didn't shake hands, three.

Joyce poured tea and I settled in, catching the stream of first impressions: all glowed with health except Russell who had had a tooth pulled the day before, couldn't speak, and communicated with a pencil and note pad; there was frequent laughter, not loud, and frequent giggling, and sometimes a whole minute went by in easy silence; dominant colours in the house were yellow, green, brown, and dark red; the living room, spied through an open door, showed a mantelpiece loaded with hockey, soccer, and swimming trophies, large Chianti bottles holding candles, lots of books, and comfortable, well-used, non-matching furniture.

No one seemed perturbed by my presence. Their community had its own throb and style and neither I nor anyone else should interrupt its workings. The Shanahans went about business pretty much as usual.

Richard was reading a newsmagazine story, which his father had recommended, on the troubles in Ireland; Ruth was looking at the sports section of a local daily and mentioned that her absolute favourite hockey player was Ken Dryden; Sheila told a long, involved story about watching Hercules on TV with Crystal, one of the cats, who ate most of her toast and who also, she said, likes potato salad and ice cream; somebody declared that she would rather not share her room with somebody else any more because the latter "burps and shrieks too much before going to sleep"; Brenda was baking a coffee cake and spent some time on Brahms's Hungarian Dance No. 5 on her trumpet; Jackie helped her mother fold some ironing; Mary was making Raggedy Ann dolls; Frances practised piano; and everybody played with Sheila whatever Sheila wanted to play.

Jim and I went for a walk around the corner from their house to an open-air hockey rink where Stephen was coaching Russell and other neighbourhood kids.

The reason for the large family is simple, Jim said. He and Joyce *like* kids. "That's why we went into education." Both were born and raised in Montreal. He came from a family of six, she from one of ten. There were a lot of teachers among their people. Fluently bilingual, Jim is a graduate of the Université de Montréal and McGill University. He started his career as a high-school math and science teacher, grew more interested in administration and worked his was up to director-general of a regional secondary-school board. Joyce also trained as an educator. Three years ago she resumed teaching English at a local high school. Raising, teaching, and enjoying children was very apparently their central preoccupation.

Watching the kids on the ice, Jim talked:

"When we grew up, procreation was the main reason for getting married. We're fortunate, you see, that we're educators. We've had the theory and the practice. There's a science to child raising and we use it. Things aren't done by trial-and-error, or haphazardly. Corporal punishment is kept to a minimum. No more than a tap, *never* a spanking, *nothing* to mortify or humiliate. It's never a waste of time to sit down and explain things to kids. I tell them, 'Everybody share and do their bit or the family won't work.' I rarely raise my voice....No, we've never really considered adoption."

Back in the house, I talked with whomever was available. Sometimes this was with much of the family present, sometimes with a single individual, and often, for some reason, up in Frances's room, which also houses Mimi the mouse. The private talks with the young Shanahans were usually prefaced with some little joke—"This is all Brenda's fault. Ha, ha." But it was unnecessary; the Shanahan youngsters weren't in the least inhibited. Each seemed to think the occasion rather interesting, even amusing. Some were asked the same questions; for instance, If you had one wish, what would it be?

Mary: "A chocolate sundae with chocolate ice cream and chocolate sauce."

Richard: "To be happy and have friends the rest of my life. That I'll never be lonely or isolated."

Frances: "To be a personal friend of all the Canadians."

Russell: "Never to have to work."

Ruth: "That Ken Dryden had a 13-year-old son so I could marry him."

Jackie: "A soda maker."

Sheila: "A house. A little small house."

This is mostly about Brenda's "live-in gang," but Jim and Joyce were its creators, and, in this regard, they told some things about themselves.

"This is maybe at the core of our family," said Jim. "When Joyce was ten, she had to have one of her kidneys removed. When we got married, three different doctors cautioned her about having children. Twice she's had infections during pregnancies…and they're dangerous. I think it says something about how much she wanted kids, knowing each time might be the clincher.

"You know, she told me the other day, 'If I stop working, I'll take in foster children.' I said, 'Oh, *no*…!' I've done my share for the country."

The parents said this about raising children:

Joyce: "If you want to communicate with them you've got to be available. I'm almost always at home at night.

"We try to live along with them. When the new math came out nine years ago we both took refresher courses.

"I try to teach them responsibility—the consequences of their decisions.

"Advice? I don't know….Love your children. Give kindness without thought of being paid back."

Jim felt the same way. "In my job I see how some kids are raised. The deformation…! There's compulsory education for everything except parenthood. Just find a mate and go to it! We had our kids because we wanted them—they don't owe us a thing.

"Rational values rank high here. Independent thinking. Don't accept something just because an adult says it. I'm prepared for them to adopt their own value systems. It's a lost cause to try to impose yours. Society *makes* them choose their own.

"Censoring of books or TV is out. They're able to handle it. And we're also always here to talk to."

"When the twins arrived," Joyce said," I was phoned by a 'twin club' to join but I said, 'No. They're no different—just next year's baby come this year!'

"Sheila *is* the last one. Actually, she was a bit of a shock. It's fun, though, having a little tag-along again. It renews you."

Sheila, may be the youngest, but she is a mighty presence. There aren't many rules in the Shanahan home, but this one is absolute: Sheila is never ever left alone. Everybody was fascinated when Joyce was pregnant with her, five years after Jackie. "But they didn't like referring to it as 'it'," Joyce recalled, "so they named 'it' Matthew— but 'it' came out Sheila!"

Brenda said it for all when she pinpointed one of the main disadvantages of living in a big family—"Too many dishes!"

The big *advantage*:

"You never need other people. For instance, the twins and me—they're my best, best, best friends."

Brenda did not, however, plan to have children herself.

"I'm going into journalism and travel," she explained. "I get ideas about things, I really like words, and I enjoy looking at people and seeing the good and the bad….I want to do more than just grow up.

"I know about the population explosion, pollution, and so on…and it makes you not want to grow up because those problems are going to be pushed into your lap. If everybody did a little it would get done. But some do so much and some nothing…."

And some random thoughts:

"The French-English situation is frustrating and silly. We've got to get together….

"Sometimes I go baby-sitting and then when I'm alone in a big house—I don't like it!

"I'd want the article to show how somebody from a big family knows better how to live together, be considerate, leave 'em alone when they're mad…."

Well, I witnessed no incident that illustrates that. By their own admission the Shanahan youngsters do quarrel, tease, and argue, and did so while I was there, but I never detected any real tension. It surely occurs, but probably not often.

Mary had different plans than older sister Brenda. "Yep, I'm going to have a big family. Mom had one and so did Grandma. I won't rush into marriage. We're Catholic so you can't get divorced. I won't marry young...around 20 or 24."

The French-English problem bothered her, too. "It's like there's an 'invisible barrier' across the schoolyard. To me it doesn't matter—as long as we can communicate in some form."

Other items:

"There are no strict rules here. If you yell it's OK, and you can run, and my parents understand you can't get high marks in *everything*.

"There's no real escape from the others in the house. You lock yourself into the bathroom, but then somebody can look through the keyhole.

"I don't like it when my parents go out. Then Stephen babysits and gets vicious, extremely vicious, and sends everybody to bed in the middle of a late-night movie!"

Vicious Stephen was a quiet, articulate six-footer. His most recent report showed an 85 percent average. He and his brother Richard had worked some of their Christmas holidays for the school caretaker, earning $34.50 and $28.50 respectively. Both are keen on sports, particularly hockey and soccer, and have travelled beyond Quebec in competitions.

Stephen said he wasn't sure yet what he would do for a living. "But it'll be something that directly involves helping other people," he said. "That I *know*."

Here is Stephen on a variety of matters:

"I'm very passive by nature. I don't fight—not even on the ice. I can't remember when I last lost my temper at home. Like my mother says, it's too dangerous, much too dangerous....If I lived in the States I would *not* go to Vietnam.

"I'm very strong against anything that even smells of nationalism. This insistence on being different is what leads to wars. I suppose I'm a world federalist.

"Drugs are cheap escape stuff. People taking them nowadays are looked on as cop-outs.

"A family like this is a burden *and* a pleasure. There's a lot of extra duties. I'm less free. And when I'm sitting at the head of the table when Dad's away, it's giving me a taste of a big family before my time. I'll wait with marrying and then not too many kids....I don't know how Dad does it!

"The family for us is very much a together thing. I'll spend my Friday night sliding with Jackie and Ruth and Russell and Sheila, rather than go to a party. The family is an end in itself. Yet for a lot of my friends it's a drag. Those they should feel closest to, they don't even know. It's almost as if people feel guilty to love their kin. *I like coming home.*

"I might adopt my children....

"I'd never put my parents in an old-age home....

"The big family has caused me to age prematurely. There's a tremendous discrepancy between me and guys my age. I don't have their enthusiasm or awe....I've largely skipped being a teenager."

And a surprise:

"Your presence," Stephen said, "has made us more aware of each other, I think. Aware that we do have a little community, that it's not just a roof over our heads."

Richard, though one year younger, is nearly as tall as his brother and his average at school was 82 percent. He got 99 percent in algebra.

"A big family," he said, "affects everybody in it differently. You learn a lot about people and how they react. I've become very quiet. Russell too, while some others have grown noisier. I guess I listen more to the other kids than give my own opinions. The younger ones like to come and tell me things."

And: "We could fix things in Canada if we tackled one problem at a time and the people in Ottawa worked more together as a team.

"Drugs don't interest me at all.

"I'll have half as large a family."

Frances, who is 45 minutes older than Mary, is very good at track and field and got 99 percent in physical fitness. Also, she may one day become the most famous, but one, of all the Shanahans.

"I intend to be a lawyer," she said, "and then a politician. I've made a bet with a friend which of us will be the first woman prime minister of Canada. My friend first wants to be an actress and if that doesn't work out, she says she can always fall back on being prime minister."

Frances had three points to make about living in a big family:

"You can form your own basketball team without asking other kids. There's always somebody to fight with....We don't get into fist fights. We're not allowed, but arguments are OK. Sometimes you can't get as much as you like—like at Christmas."

And she had views on women's lib, ambition, parenthood, and war:

"When I get married I'm keeping my own name....I'm setting my aims high so I'll get high....I doubt I'll have kids because it'll interfere with my career. If I had a family I'd have to stay in—kids don't grow up well if at least one parent isn't home. To prevent war everybody might have to learn to speak Esperanto."

One fine aspect of being in a large family, said Jackie, while drying dishes, is that "On your birthday when you have a whole bunch of brothers and sisters you get lots of presents."

Also: "If Mom and Dad are busy and you're reading a book and you want to ask something you can ask one of the older guys and he'll tell you."

Not so good: "In summer when we go on the swing there's only room for two and there's a big fight. And when Mom goes shopping she can't bring *everybody*."

Still: "I'll have a family of around six."

Russell, the youngest boy, didn't say much, mostly because of the painful hole in his mouth. It had taken ten minutes to get the tooth out, he wrote, and it hurt, yes. Other data: he might become a lawyer or a hockey player; disliked school; enjoyed vanilla ice cream; took the garbage out often; would rather be in a large family of only boys; and liked hockey, soccer, swimming, and eating.

Yes, what *about* food?

"I buy at the corner grocery," said Joyce. "I like the service, the credit, and it's delivered. You don't really save at big stores. In an average week I might buy 63 quarts of milk, four pounds of butter, 15 loaves of bread, three dozen eggs, two-and-a-half pounds of bacon, three dozen oranges, and nine 48-ounce cans of fruit juice.

Every two weeks I get 25 pounds of potatoes and 20 pounds of detergent; and every six weeks, 20 pounds of rolled oats. Apples we buy by the bushel and meat by the side. Groceries come to $450 a month, school lunches, $24."

Jim: "I make $20,000 a year and Joyce about another $7,000. We're fortunate to have that much....I wonder, sometimes, if I'm perpetuating a system that is at least inequitable. Some of the kids already challenge me on this."

Joyce: "I hate money and I don't handle it well. Most clothes shopping I do from catalogues; it's easier. Clothes cost about $75 a month, school transportation, $30, music lessons, $30, and day care for Sheila, $72. The oil bill is $450 a year. Every two weeks I get a cleaning lady in for a day and that's $20."

Surveys on four subjects were taken among the family, one of which didn't pan out—routines.

"There aren't any, really," said Joyce. "We don't like rules. For instance, I prepare meals on the *children's* schedules—hockey games and so on—not mine. It's not a business we're running—it's a home."

The other three were on family favourites:

TV programs: *Hockey Night in Canada, Wonderful World of Disney, Get Smart, Lassie, Reach for the Top, Sesame Street,* CBC specials like *Elizabeth R, Weekend, Friday Night Movie, Star Trek.*

Activity: Having visitors and/or parties.

Traditions: Sunday Mass; summer vacation at Grandma's cottage; Sunday dinner; Christmas visits to each set of grandparents; birthday suppers; watching boys' soccer matches; annual winter outings up north complete with hamburgers; and the yearly trip to Long Island to visit great-uncle Frank, a retired linotype operator of the *New York Post,* whose house the family takes over while he happily bunks in the basement.

Ruth, the hockey fan, had several pertinent things to say as well as some questions of her own: "No, I don't want a big family—just six. Too much work and I'd have to cook spaghetti in a big pot. I'll get engaged when I'm 19, married at 20.

"Are *you* from a large family?

"The dishes aren't so bad. There are lots of others so you get a break sometimes. You're also never the only person raking the back yard. And people admire you when you say, 'I have three brothers and five sisters.' They say. 'Oh, my goodness!' But we're too crowded at the dinner table and in front of the TV.

"Have you ever met Ken Dryden?

"I'd like to live where there's no commotion, no wars, no pollution, no bad hockey teams...maybe New Brunswick.

"I don't know how Mom keeps her temper....She's *screaming* at us and then the phone rings and she just wipes it away and says, 'Hellooo?'

"Does *Weekend Magazine* come out in Kentucky?"

Before it's finally Sheila's turn, there was one other question put to most of the Shanahans: if you were on live TV and given 30 seconds to say something to Canada, what would it be?

Brenda and Mary: "Like Anne Murray sings, 'Canada stand together, understand together.'"

Joyce: "Accept what you can't change—and do the best you can."

Richard: "Try and understand the other guy's problems before you start complaining about yours."

Frances: "If you remember my name 40 years from now—vote for me!"

Russell: "Fight pollution!"

Jim: "Try to accomplish well whatever you undertake. This applies as much to child rearing as to medicine or plumbing. Your family may in the long run be your most important contribution."

Ruth: "Ken Dryden, I wish you had a son!"

Stephen: "Stop, look, and listen to the guy beside you."

Jackie: "Hello....I've never been on TV before....I hope you have a nice day....If you're going on a trip, I hope you have a good trip....Maybe I'll say a few jokes....I'm sending in for this book of 101 elephant jokes...."

But Sheila was the one. In about three decades she's bound to be in *Weekend* again. Same kind of story, too. She was asked four hard, fast questions:

"You going to be a mommy?"

She nodded.

"Will you have babies?"

She nodded again.
"How many girls?"
She held up five fingers.
"How many boys?"
And she held up ten fingers!

Chapter 6

Fastest Bar in the East

It's 4:40 PM in Montreal. The year is 1969, and the CN's Rapido is taking off for Toronto. Three hundred and thirty-five Quebec and Ontario miles in five hours, every day of the week. From the heart of one town to the heart of the other. No bother, no fuss. Climb aboard, find a seat, heave up the baggage, take off your coat, hang it up....No, take it down, fold it, and put it on your seat so you know you can always come back—and start walking. You're in a coach in the back of the train and it's a long tramp, car in, car out, past all the people in the seats, through the dining car. Keep going. It's way up front behind the locomotive.

Others are marching the same trail. Keep going. Not to panic. There, a car length away, it beckons, the marvelous orange paint all over the outside door, and that glorious international word, big and bold—BISTRO. Open the door and enter a darkish orange world; you're in the belly of an orange whale. And if five hours of roaring through this bit of Canada still seems long, forget it. You're in the fastest bar in the east. (Because of Ontario's licensing laws, passengers on the Rapido have to do without the Bistro on Sundays.)

Get a seat now, if possible near the piano. (Yes, there's a piano in the whale.) Next: a drink. Already most of the 66 seats are filled with people with rosy, glowing faces from the red-shaded lamps along the orange and red walls. On the ceiling are a couple of authentic-looking brass gaslights and two spotlights glaring at the piano. Along the walls are posters of early movie greats: Charlie Chaplin, Rudolph Valentino, Douglas Fairbanks, Sr, Laurel and Hardy, Theda Bara, and Pola Negri. The little round table you're sitting at is screwed to the floor. There's not a window in the place.

You're moving now, rolling out, forgetting a little of what you're leaving, not thinking a lot of what's ahead. How can you? You're meeting Andy, a consulting engineer, and Janis, a legal secretary, who was sitting next to Andy in the coach and whom he's now telling: "Whew! Got here just in the nick of time." And there's Jackie in a purple blouse with a gigantic pointed collar and grey bell-bottomed pants. She's blonde and 21 and she is, she says, an intermediate clerk, and she's coming from a holiday with her girlfriend, Diana, who's an executive secretary, and they had this really wild time. Diana is dark-haired and 23 in a yellow blouse, a black velvet vest, and grey bell-bottomed pants. They both order rye and ginger ale, and Janis and Andy order rum and ginger ale.

Andy leans back, folds his hands across his stomach and says:

"This, let me tell you, is the only way to fly." And he laughs.

Jackie says: "I call it the Bistro train, not the Rapido anymore." Jackie has been this way before.

And so has Adrian McCrea who is squeezing in behind the piano. (It's Adrian, that is, if you're going west today; if you're going east, it's Lorna Kolodey, a blonde pianist. Tomorrow it's the other way around.)

Adrian is "a bit over 40," covers his thick white hair with a flat straw hat, and sports a green vest and arm braces. He used to have his own orchestra, but now he plays a mean honky-tonk piano and is the most travelled sing-along star, maybe in the world. He has been with the car since it started in May last year.

"Hi!" says Adrian. "Welcome to the bouncing or balancing bistro, or the orange submarine, or our perambulating pub." He plays a few bars of "It's a Long Way to Tipperary." "When you get your elbows properly bent we'll do a little singing."

A man in a sport shirt at the table across promptly starts bellowing along. Not the words, just the tune—"Yah-de-dah-dah-dee-dah-de-dah-dah." All the way, he will bellow, cheer, and clap after every song, drink beer without pause, and at journey's end put on his jacket and walk out, steady as a rock.

Adrian plays quiet songs for a while, old-time songs, and gets to know the people. There are two microphones, one for him and one detachable in case somebody gets inspired. And somebody will.

"Everybody happy here?" asks the waiter in his yellow vest with black buttons.

You're clickety-clacking at least 65 miles per hour now, but do you know it? No, because you're in an orange whale and about half your friends are now singing a still fairly subdued, "Roll Out the Barrel." The other half is watching, getting the feel of the place. The girl across the aisle in the severe beige suite, she's watching, and she's not comfortable. At the nice ladies' college she attends…. Well, really, should people let go like that man in the sport shirt? "Yah-de-dah-de-dah-dee-dah!" ("Take Me Out to the Ball Game.") She's watching him, not smiling at all. But by 7:30, believe me, exactly, she was sitting at his table, and he was old enough to be her father, too, bellowing "Sweet Georgia Brown"— "Yah-de-dah-dah."

About this time a pretty, middle-aged lady—all the ladies are pretty—in a brown dress comes in, and there's no seat, so a group of noisy young guys make room for her at their table and order her a drink. One of them, a chubby fellow, puts his arm around her shoulder. His friends smile at her, so she lets his arm be.

In the corner near the bar, sits a man with a completely bald head and a great curling moustache. His features are Mongolian, and he may well be a spy.

In the midst of "I've Been Working on the Railroad," Jackie says: "This is just like going out. It's funny, everybody is so free."

Which is certainly true for Pat, another secretary, from Halifax. Pat's been sitting next to the piano, and suddenly she gets up, grabs the detachable mike and right in front of all those people goes into "April Showers." She is 20, and has never been on this train before. Nothing shy about Pat. Now with feeling, "This Land Is My Land," and with more feeling, "Dear Old Nova Scotia." She should be on TV!

Andy says it again: "This is the only way to fly!"

From Pat, the mike goes to John, who is so good, people would almost like to stop their own singing and listen. But they don't. "The Band Played On," "Take Me Out to the Ball Game" (again), "Michael Row the Boat Ashore." The Mongolian is not singing. He's having a drink, though. Probably vodka.

A young man named Karl somehow squeezes in beside Jackie. He asks her: "Will you buy me a beer?"

Jackie says: "No."

Other stars take their turn at the mike. A pretty lady in a pink spring suit—"Clementine"; Andy himself—"Hang Up the Washing on the Siegfried Line," "Take Me Out to the Ball Game" (again); sure enough, the middle-aged lady in the brown suit— "When Irish Eyes Are Smiling." A French girl—"Alouette"; two guys from the noisy group—"Yes Sir, That's My Baby"; and back to Pat—"Never On Sunday," and "Havah Nagilah."

Diana says to no one in particular: "I just want to do my own thing."

Jackie says: "I'm going to ask them to sing 'Ca-na-da.'"

And they do, and if there's one song that turns them on in this shaking, rattling old railroad car, it's "Ca-na-da!" If we liked each other and ourselves before, we sure do so now. This is our song. "Ca-na-da!" Pat and John are on the mike, Jackie is standing on her seat conducting (and is told to get right down) and in the aisle are the man in the sport shirt and the girl from the ladies' college, bellowing. The Mongolian is singing, too. For just a few moments you can't hear the noise of the train at all....

Last call comes around. You'll be in Toronto in a few minutes. Now you think a little of what is ahead there. The last words Adrian says before he closes the piano are: "If you ever have occasion to travel this way again, be damn sure you travel this way—it is the only way to fly!"

And then there was the man from St Louis who, sometime during the evening told you what he thought of this train ride. It took him a minute and a half and he used the word fabulous, 11 times exactly.

Maybe it is the only way to fly.

Chapter 7

No Mail for Roderick Yooya

In Stony Rapids, Saskatchewan, there are people, dogs, trucks, snowmobiles, radios, saws, and guns, but often, even in the middle of the day, it is so still that the silence sings. To make a tiny sound then, like the squeak of a boot on the snow, is almost sacrilegious.

In Stony Rapids, the world is very far away—Prince Albert, 500 miles south, Uranium City on Lake Athabasca, 100 miles west, the Northwest Territories, 50 miles north. From the air, in late March, 1970, it's a small clutch of buildings where nothing moves in the snow. The land around has no end—white rivers, vast stretches of pine and spruce and sleeping lakes. Unless you're flying low, you miss it.

In Stony Rapids live 138 people. Chippewayan Indians, Métis, and a handful of whites. On any Monday or Wednesday, when the DC-3 from Prince Albert delivers the mail, most of them will make their way to the Hudson's Bay store. The Bay is also the post office, and if there is a place where the action is in Stony Rapids, this is it.

One of the first to ask if there's mail for him is Roderick Yooya. He must be the saddest-looking man in town. He hangs around the store all day, every day, usually sitting in the corner by the front door on a stand-up ashtray. There's a rip in the back of his cloth cap and a tuft of graying, dry hair sticks out. His clothes are rumpled and greasy. He smokes factory-made cigarettes, chews gum, and drinks a lot of orange pop. He rarely talks to anyone. He's said to be in his early 50s. His mouth curves downward, and his black slanted eyes have no life at all.

When the store is closed, Roderick stays home. He lives a couple of miles out of town in one of half a dozen shacks scattered about a treeless slab of land. There are no trees because they've all been burned for firewood. Now there's no protection at all from the wind, and each year the residents must travel further for wood. Most of the shacks look no bigger than one-car garages and house families of six or eight or more. There is no electricity and water is fetched from a hole in the lake ice. In the bare main room, Roderick sits rooted at a stained little table. Sometimes he listens to the transistor radio. Sometimes he plays cards for long hours with other men.

There never is any mail for Roderick, and anyway, he can't read.

In Stony Rapids, there seem to be a lot like him, though none quite as sad looking. When the warm weather comes, there'll be a few American fishermen to guide, some survey lines to cut maybe, but right now just about everybody seems to be living off family allowance, or unemployment insurance, or income tax returns, or Indian Affairs handouts. And if there is this money, which will keep you alive, why go out and hunt, or trap, or fish, or do much of anything? So they play cards, or hang around the store, talking low and little, wandering through the aisles between the counters and shelves, looking at the merchandise they've seen a hundred times before. If they need five gallons of coal oil in a week, they'll buy one gallon a day. Usually the men visit in the morning, the women and children in the afternoon. At the end of the day, the floor is littered with butts, candy wrappers, and empty orange pop cans.

In Stony Rapids, there are two ladies who would cheer up any place. Old and bent and wiry, in long skirts and thick, brown stockings, Rosalie and Esther feel they practically own the store. Rosalie smokes a pipe, Esther cigarettes. Both chew a lot of gum. Almost anything that happens is worth a cackle or a whisper. Now they're in stitches at store manager Garth Yeomans, six feet two, 210 pounds carefully setting out silk panties. They were disappointed last week when no new dresses came for Easter because of the Montreal mail strike. Esther holds up a sweatshirt with "Look That Up in Your Funk and Wagnalls" on the front. Rosalie follows with a "You Bet Your Sweet Bippie." A clutch of teenagers by the canned goods watches Esther cut up trying on a yellow baseball cap. Now they all have to try the caps, and the sweaters, and the new cowboy hats. There's mild roughhousing, but Garth knows better than to break it up. Soon they're quiet again. One girl in silk turquoise gloves buys a can of apple juice and drinks it down.

The store is a large, square room with pale green and beige furnishings. It's warm and lit by ten light bulbs. Some 1,800 different items are on display here. Garth, at 22, seems young to run such an enterprise. But since he came up from Edmonton at 18 he's clerked in and managed stores in Fort Simpson, Rae, Reindeer Station, Inuvik, Snowdrift, Hay River, Arctic River, and Keg River. "I came up to make big money and get out," he says. "I'm still here, four years later, trying to make big money and get out." He seems suited to the country: big, calm, self-sufficient. He's also a good cook.

In Stony Rapids, it's been a bad winter. The caribou haven't come south very far from the Barrens, and there's been little meat. In the old days there would have been starvation; today there is malnutrition. The caribou is like potatoes or bread here. Life isn't good without caribou.

Boniface Mercredi, who has clerked in the store for 30 years, says that the most exciting times of his life have always been hunting caribou. "You come right near them into the wind," he says, "and you can yell and whistle and wave your arms and they just stand watching. They throw up their heads like this—Sniffffff! It is the most beautiful thing in the world."

Boniface is worried about Stony Rapids' boys and girls, the children of the Sayazies, McDonalds, Robillards, Kaysons, Toutsaints, and Yooyas.

"This is the North country, you know," he explains, "but in the school they don't learn kids about North country. They don't learn to fish or hunt. Without welfare, they'd die. The old people, like me, *we* know. We don't die. I always eat meat, all winter, because my boys and I catch rabbits. But the young people, they don't know...."

Two white men come in for their mail: Jim Good and Gordon Rowan.

Jim is the radio operator for the Saskatchewan department of natural resources, and he has been up here since 1959. He tells about fixing plane transportation for a little boy with meningitis this morning. There have been 12 cases in the area this winter. Jim hunts a lot, moose mostly. "One big one gives me $400 worth of meat. I prefer it to beef." He gets three weeks' holidays but often doesn't bother taking them. He has a wife and four kids. From Winnipeg originally, Jim has been in and around the North since 1948. "I wouldn't want to live in the city even a little bit," he says.

Gordon and his wife Zinnia run the Norcanair office. He's off in the Beaver a lot, flying nurses, trappers, prospectors, tourists, while she does the paperwork. They came in less than a year ago. Before that he was crop dusting and firefighting around Calgary. Gordon says that what he loves about flying here is that "it's different every time you put her up, and every time you bring her down." He also says that he likes the Indians. "You could make some of your best friends of them if you just paid attention to them as if they were human beings."

In Stony Rapids, and in Black Lake, a similar, small community 16 miles east, few of the whites talk like that about the Indians. Among themselves they may call them yo-yos, knickknacks, bows and arrows. The most common term is "natives," as in: "It's a good idea to stay neutral with the natives—familiarity breeds contempt," or, "The natives aren't better or worse than we are—just different." (There's also one in a book called *Northern Survival* prepared by the federal department of Indian Affairs and Northern Development, published in 1969. On page 18 there's this heading: "Diseases present in natives and animals that may be transmitted to man.") The whites fret about the Indians, they theorize about them, they nurse them, teach them, but they don't seem to like them a lot. The whites live in well-built homes with hot and cold running water, electricity, and proper heating. Many are earning more money than they would down south. As a consequence, they seem to be living in cocoons, quite unrelated to the lives of the people most them are up here to serve. It's debatable how useful they are.

All of which probably doesn't matter much to Leon Medal, who has just come in with his dogs from a month's trapping. He lives in the bush with his family, 25 miles west of here. He is said to be a good trapper, and he's teaching his sons to trap. He brings in 13 lynx and four beavers. Garth snaps the furs to make the hair stand up and measures them. Leon earns $208 this day. In a winter he'll make between $800 and $900. He looks fit, the skin on his face is tight over the bones and there's a glow to it. He says that lynx will not struggle in a trap, that once caught they go completely still. The old people say that if you're trapped in a tree you can put a forked stick to a lynx's throat and it won't move. If properly bled its meat tastes like chicken. But now Leon has to go. There's coal oil to buy, and flour, tea, sugar, and salt, and he has relatives to visit.

Chief Louis Chicken, who lives in Black Lake, has caught a ride into town. The Black Lake store ran out of snuff, and he's badly in need. The chief is an elderly, frail man who smiles a lot. He carries an empty orange-pop can to spit in. It's not known exactly how much power Louis Chicken wields among his people. He has, however, done much pressing in the past for increased handouts. The whites kid him a lot.

In Stony Rapids, they show movies on Wednesday and Saturday nights. Westerns and Elvis Presley films are the most popular. The cowboys are always the heroes. The popcorn is 15 cents for a large bag. They always laugh at the most dramatic moments—Hollywood's notion of drama in the starkness of Stony Rapids is a bit ludicrous. And they laugh when the stars kiss. But last Saturday the wooden benches were nearly empty. For one thing, it was just one of those beach-party films, and, for another, Easter Sunday was the next day and Father Jean Porte was holding midnight Mass in Black Lake.

A lot of us that night caught a ride to the church with Garth in the open pickup. Two young guys were drunk and shouting a lot and fooling around with the girls in the back. It got so bad, or good, one of the girls screeched, "C'mon John, you know that you're not supposed to bite!" It was 20 below and the Northern Lights were dancing. Exactly halfway the truck careened off the icy road into a snow bank. The two young men started cursing and name calling, especially at Garth the driver. One of them yelled: "You—white! Get this—thing outta here, you—white!" Garth ignored them and grabbed a shovel. Others waded into the snow to break off branches to put under the back wheels. Two women with babies sat in the cabin, which was getting cold. Then one of the drunks, as big as Garth himself, lunged at him. Garth dropped the shovel, grabbed the man by the throat, lifted him up and plunged him deep into the snow, head first. After a moment he let go, not saying a word, and went back to shovelling. The young fellow stumbled away. In the scuffle he had cut his hand and blood oozed out until his friend tied it up with a handkerchief. Then the young man, leaning over the fender, vomited into the snow. The truck was back on the road in 45 minutes. When Mass began everybody was present, men on the left, women on the right, and on their knees.

Father Porte has been in the area—first Stony Rapids then Black Lake—for 23 years. He is from Lyon, France. He speaks fluent Chippewayan, and his sermons are mostly in that language. He knows the people here better than anyone else. Religion is a serious matter to them and he has much influence. He respects the Indians. But no, he said, he had never had personal friends among them.

A young American anthropologist who lives among the Indians at Black Lake, also has that problem. But Stephen Sharp, who is studying the Chippewayans for his PhD, is working to remedy it. The Indians probably thought of him as a fool and a clown, he said. He hardly associated with the whites, but clearly he didn't make a good Indian either. He didn't even know how to chop wood properly. He looked tired and said he had already lost 70 pounds. But he was never without company. People are always wandering in for coffee. When the ice breaks he plans to move into the bush with one family and try to learn something of their hunting and fishing skills. "I'm thinking of a lifetime commitment," he said. "There's too much good here to just leave and forget."

In Stony Rapids, there's an RCMP post, a hospital, an oil depot, a little school, all staffed by people from the south. Friendly, hospitable people, who have a lot to say to someone trying to get a taste of what life's like in a small northern town. But they are people who come and go. The Mercredis, McDonalds, Robillards, Kaysons, Toutsaints, and Sayazies, they stay.

Roderick Yooya stays, too. And when the store closes at night he shuffles home in the silence.

Somebody should write him a letter.

[NOTE: A week or so after this story came out, letters started arriving for Roderick Yooya, sacks full of them, from all over the country.]

"It's the Classic Peasant System— Perpetual Debt to the Store."

Stephen Sharp, 25, a graduate in anthropology from Duke University in North Carolina, lives in a one-room shack in the village of Black Lake near Stony Rapids. It has a population of about 500, mostly Chippewayan Indians and Métis. Stephen has been up four months and plans to stay another eight, studying the Indians for his doctorate. Here are some of his observations:

- I met one young white man here who said pointblank: "Being white makes me smarter, morally superior, and better than any—Indian."

- If a medical team had come in here in January they would have found over 90 percent of the children suffering from malnutrition....A hell of a lot are suffering from it now.

- Dental care is nonexistent. If you complain enough, you can go up to Uranium City for half a day and get your teeth pulled. The thought of permanent molars being pulled out of 16-year-olds....

- After 300 years of raping the Indian, you'd think Hudson's Bay would be willing to marry the old girl. It essentially takes and gives nothing back. Its prices are high. Its credit operation is very much the classical peasant system—perpetual debt to the store.

- I'd like to see four or five of those women-liberation types up here for a summer, and one or two Black Panthers.

- There seems to be a systematic desire to draw the Indians into little ghettoes and let them sit there.

- I have no illusions about who is going to win if it's a toss-up between oil, uranium, or the Indians. Western civilization has a perfect track record so far.

"The First Thing They Should Do Here Is Stop the Relief."

Father Porte, who is the Roman Catholic priest for Stony Rapids and Black Lake, knew neither Chippewayan nor English when he came to the area from France, 23 years ago. He mastered the first in three years and only then set about learning the second. He probably knows more about the people in the two communities than any other white man. Here are some of the things he says about them:

- With 500, we are already too many in Black Lake. Each year they must go farther away to hunt, to fish, for wood. There are some families that go away and don't come back for a whole year.

- I like the Indians. But I believe we are different from them. Not superior. My right hand is not my left hand, but they work together.

- Anybody who thinks he is above the Indian should take five pounds of lard, 20 shells, his 30-30, and go in the bush from September till Easter—if he comes back, he can talk.

- The caribou herds are diminishing. The government has said it is the wolves, the rapids, nature. The Indian laughs. Were there not wolves and rapids 50 years ago? The government knows what's happened, but isn't telling. Radioactivity in the Barrens. Maybe the females went sterile or something like that.

- The first thing they should do here is stop the relief. In 23 years I see many families go down. They were good trappers, now they are not. Why? If you have three or four children, you get $250 a month, plus family allowance. But a man can never say this is mine. So when you reduce

a man so he has to bark just to get his fish, what is he?
A dog.

- They come to church because of fear of God. Of course,
they are closer to nature and they can see how powerful He
could be. For the last five years there have been no slow
deaths for men—all sudden deaths. Shooting accidents,
drownings, heart attacks. That makes them a little bit
scared.

- They are more generous than white people. If my jeep gets
stuck tonight in the snow, there would be ten dog sleighs
to pull me out in a few minutes.

Chapter 8

A Book Lover's Bookstore

The place is worth a book, of course. It's pure Canadiana. So many of the greats of this country have passed through here— either live or in print—and still do, that there's a smell of history.

Albert Britnell, an Englishman from the Yorkshire village of Chinnor, founded this business in 1893 in Toronto. "Browsing" means grazing, and he coined the phrase, despite the purists, "Come in and browse around."

Albert's son Roy, 69 [1970], started work in the shop at 16. He had always wanted to be a lawyer; instead, he became a master bookseller and has no regrets whatever. A driving, ebullient man, whose second passion after books is politics, he shaped and worked the little enterprise into the finest bookshop in Canada, possibly in North America. (The store also does good business: on a day during the peak of Christmas season, Britnell's will sell 2,000 cloth-bound books and take in 200 special orders.)

In 1956, the younger of Roy's two sons, Barry, 33, joined his father. Barry now owns the place, but he and Roy run it together. They do so, as Barry says, "by breaking our necks trying to get people the books they want."

"*Gulliver's Travels*," said the man.

"Yes, sir," said the clerk. She looked first on one shelf, then another. She climbed on a stool so she could reach the top shelf. She made her way to the rear where the paperbacks are. She consulted a list and then a catalogue. She checked the secondhand books. Finally she went upstairs and checked the stockroom. Success! *Gulliver's Travels* in a nice blue dust jacket.

"I want it in red," said the man.

The Albert Britnell Book Shop is a two-storey brick building with a modest sign out front near the corner of Yonge and Bloor Streets. Roy built it in 1928. (He had six people working for him that year; Christmas 1969 there were 75.) The furnishings are mostly gumwood with walnut finish, and there's an old cash register that rings loudly.

One reason for Britnell's reputation is that it has the largest selection of books in stock in the country. Another reason is a tradition of service: if the book you want is not in stock, they will write, telephone, cable, or advertise in trade publications, until they get it. And it doesn't matter if it costs 80 cents or $8, the price stays the same. Maybe that's why Sir Wilfred Laurier bought his books here. And William Lyon Mackenzie King, Vincent Massey, Joey Smallwood, A.Y. Jackson, Lorne Greene, the Princess of Leiningen, Christopher Morley, Pierre Berton, Mrs E.P. Taylor, Marshall McLuhan, Lister Sinclair, a former Queen of Bulgaria, Nathan Cohen, Leonard Brockington, Arthur Hailey, Johnny Wayne, Frank Shuster, Mrs John Diefenbaker, Wyndham Lewis, Edmund Wilson, Morton Shulman, and I.

Among other browsers in snow-wet overcoats, I shuffle through narrow aisles between the tables and racks bursting with books. There's a hum of low voices. I remember that each day I spent here, working in the shipping room 15 years ago, made the world a little larger for me, a little more interesting.

Britnell's clerks (my mother is one)—they are all ladies, and some have been here for years—say slightly incredible things, like:

"This place envelops you. You get in and you never want to get out."

"You dress, you eat, you live for Britnell's."

"I don't work for a bookstore—I work for *Britnell's*."

Barry Britnell himself is at a loss to explain this attitude.

"Wages could be better," he says, "and the hours."

The secret is probably in the Britnells' own approach to the work—they live it. They care about every detail. They work long hours, six days a week, take short holidays, if at all, have no real outside hobbies. And most of the time they seem to be thoroughly enjoying themselves. They love books, they say, though a lot of their reading is publishers' catalogues and reviews.

Both father and son talk at length on the importance of a large stock, good service, a happy staff—but never about profits. I doubt if anyone in the shop has ever heard profits discussed. Of course, it's their own affair, but also, somehow, they give an impression they're not always thinking about profits.

Roy, who speaks with half a century of book selling behind him, says it all for both of them: "I enjoy books. I enjoy handling books. And I enjoy meeting people."

———◆·◆·◆———

A poll among the staff reveals that the book they got the most kick out of selling was *Canada: Year of the Land* by the National Film Board.

A Britnell clerk never calls another to the phone if she's busy with a client; she politely disengages herself from a customer who is more intent on conversation than her help; when showing a book she hands it to the customer and lets him look at it himself; she never converses with another clerk while she's making change; when a customer wants to look around, she doesn't follow him about, just keeps an eye on him to give help when it's needed; she's as pleasant on the telephone as when she's facing a customer; if she's sitting down when a customer comes in, she rises; and she never, never appears in the shop with liquor on her breath.

She was in her late 20s and her hair was combed and sprayed to perfection. Her eyes darted for help among the Saturday crowd of browsers. A saleslady approached.

"Yes, madam?"

"*How to Catch and Hold a Man,*" she blurted out.

"I beg your pardon?"

"*How to Catch and Hold a Man.* It's a book."

"Oh yes, of course. If you'll just wait here, I'll see if we have a copy."

The customer picked up a book at random, riffled the pages, put it down. She picked up another one.

"I'm sorry," said the clerk, coming back. "We don't seem to have it in stock. But I can call the publisher first thing Monday...."

"No," sighed the lady with the hairdo. "Don't bother—Monday will be too late."

I start to count book titles on the 336 shelves and ten tables in the shop. Children's books—1,500, give or take a few; drinks—47; collecting—188; cookbooks—212; fine arts—1,383. And then I give up.

Harold, who has run the shipping room for 35 years, will start in about a month again uttering his dark daily warning: "Christmas is coming." He and his assistants mail books to every part of Canada, the United States, Britain, most countries in Europe, Rhodesia, Nigeria, India, Pakistan, Malaysia, Australia, New Zealand, and Brazil.

Barry Britnell is a good-humoured, quiet, unflappable man. He believes operating a bookshop is "a worthwhile thing to do. The community would sorely miss it if it weren't there."

Roy Britnell: "Others have contributed more than I. My father for whom I began working, my son Barry for whom I ended up working, my lawyer son David who, so far, has kept me out of trouble, a most understanding wife, a wonderful staff, a fine clientele, and the aid of my publisher friends."

It's easy to miss the shop on this busy corner in Toronto. The store windows are small and a little old-fashioned. Pity, now that finally something of mine—this magazine piece—may be displayed there.

Chapter 9

"Fish Aren't Born to Feel Sorry For"

Salt spray whips my hip boots, wind cuts through to my thermal underwear. I stumble trying to stay on my feet and the churning below my rib cage won't stop. And then I think of something I shouldn't think about this cold, stormy morning on the Atlantic Ocean in mid-winter [1970]. I think of the breakfast I had....

I am ten miles out of Port Mouton on Nova Scotia's south shore aboard the *Elaine and Sisters*, a 39-foot Cape Island longliner. For 15 days straight, I've been told, there's been rain and a strong east wind. No one can remember her being so "sickly" for so long at this time of year.

Lockie Burgess shuts off the motor. He's stocky, 52 years old, and the skin of his neck is weather-creased in squares. The thump of the six-cylinder diesel dies, and now there's only the sound of the wind and the rain and the sea.

"We'll do some jigging!" shouts Lockie.

I nod.

He looks at me. "You sick?"

I nod again.

I suspect Lockie is maybe a little pleased this isn't a day when she's fine and the sun is shining. I've been staying with him and his family for four days trying to get some idea of what a fisherman's life is like, and so far it's been all talk. But this little boat, this toy, pitching and rolling at the will of the black foaming water, is real.

As a favour, Lockie took me out today, Sunday, to watch them getting the mackerel out of the nets. He has 21 tubs of baited trawl waiting in the fish plant's icehouse, but she's just been too rough to go out. And now he won't go out any more until lobstering starts. He still has 32 of his 100 traps to build and all his buoy line to splice, and lobster pays $1 a pound.

Lockie lets out a plastic line tied to a steel silver fish with two hooks in its tail. He lets down until he hits bottom then pulls her up a few yards. Jigging is letting go an arm's length and then hauling her back fast. He jigs once and brings in a four-pound codfish. He jigs again. A nine-pounder. I try it now. I jig and I jig, and nothing happens.

Lockie is in the cabin talking on the "talking machine." The response comes over in a metallic jabber—an eerie sound. I keep jigging.

"Did you let down all the way?" he asks stepping back on deck. I nod.

He takes the line, lets go another 15 feet, and hands it back. "You didn't," he says.

I jig, and now there's a tug. A little tug. I start pulling her in, hand over hand, and up it comes jumping and flapping its tail. A monster!

"Two or three pounds," says Lockie.

He catches five more, and I one. A big wave falls away and we see another boat coming at us. Five men in oilskins are bent over pulling in a net and untangling mackerel from it. They pay no attention to us. The occasional dogfish is banged on the head and heaved back into the water. Lockie starts the motor and moves in closer.

"Sick!" he shouts, pointing at me.

Now the five fishermen look up.

"Sick, eh?" one yells. I nod.

They turn back to their work, absorbed again. We watch them for a while until Lockie decides we've been out long enough and turns the *Elaine* away.

We slip and slide and jump. I climb around the boat trying to find one tiny spot that's stationary. Suddenly Lockie is holding a banana in his hand, peeling it.

"You want some?"

I turn and lean far over starboard.

———◆•◆———

The *Elaine and Sisters* is moored to the causeway in the bay. Port Mouton, 12 miles southwest of Liverpool in Queen's County, only shows on detailed maps of Canada. The Indians called it Wolugumkook or "hole in the river." In 1604, the French explorer de Monts sailed in and named it Port Mouton when one of his precious load of sheep fell overboard. (*Mouton* is French for sheep.)

Lockie lives a five-minute drive away in South West Port Mouton, a fishing community of 43 families with 16 telephones. He was born and raised in a house 500 yards away from where he lives now, just up from the beach.

With quick slashes he's dressing our nine fish for salting. Seagulls swoop in for the heads and guts.

It took me several hours the first day to learn to understand Lockie. They speak English a little differently in South West Port M'toon: Dead is *did*, and so is dad; bed is *bid*; nothing is *naathin*; fine is *foine*; card is *cod* and cod is *cood*; and so on. But he was patient with me. He was also a bit reserved at first, but his Maritime friendliness soon won out. He doesn't talk easily, though, or a lot.

Lockie was 12 when he first went to sea. At 14 he was fishing full time with his father and brothers. There were 14 in the family, and six of the eight boys became fishermen. At 21 Lockie married a girl from his village, and he and Irene have eight children—Sandra, 30, Carol, 27, Patrick, 24, Oressa, 22, Faye, 18, Jo-Anne, 16, Mac, 13, Gordon, ten—and five grandchildren.

"Even after I was married I tried going back to school," he told me one night after supper. "I was in grade nine, but I knew as much as the teacher—and she didn't know nothing. Next year I tried again. Same thing. I *had* to quit. They just didn't have any teachers around here in those days that had any more learning than I did."

For a while, in his early 20s, when Sandra had already come, Lockie peddled fish around the county for his father at $1 a day.

One reason they managed then was that they had already bought—for $200—the two-storey, four-bedroom house they live in now.

But in summer he was off to Cape Breton, swordfishing. Those were the days. Eight-week trips. Big pay. And Lockie was always the striker. With his mates up in the rigging, and he with the harpoon in the stand jutting from the bow, they patrolled the sea searching for the fins. The biggest he ever stuck weighed 730 pounds dressed. Once he made $1,800 in six weeks. He stopped off in Glace Bay and bought blankets and all sorts of things for the house, and for Irene $15 worth of black lace underwear and a $37 watch. She was very pleased with the watch.

At the beginning of the '50s he had saved enough to buy the *Blanche MK*, a 46-footer. He didn't change her name because he believes that can put a jinx on a boat. It's his only superstition. He laughs at some fishermen in the area who threaten to throw a man overboard if he says "pig" at sea, or won't let him aboard at all if he's not wearing white socks.

In 1953 the *Blanche MK*'s motor exploded while in harbour and she went down with most of the gear. His second boat he lost the next year when she smashed up coming in from a storm. About the same thing happened to his third boat the year after that.

Lockie stopped catching fish and went back to peddling them. For four years he made steady money. Then he bought his fourth boat.

"He's too independent," explained Irene that night. "He can't take any kind of orders. And, well, I guess the sea is in his blood."

The *Pat and Jo-Anne* was the first new boat Lockie ever owned. And then he lost her, too....

Lockie: "It was '61, I think. December 27, anyway, and she was moored in South West Bay half a mile from here. The gale came in at 100 miles. You could stand right out on the wind that night."

Irene: "We went down in the car and saw it. Lockie put the car lights on her."

Lockie: "She landed near the beach, dragging her mooring, but she didn't come right ashore—she hung back. And when she turned around on her side she worked over to the rocks....If there'd been any way I could've got out to her and cut her away from the mooring, she would've come right on the beach....She wouldn't have hurt at all. I felt pretty bad."

Irene: "I cried."

Lockie: "I think I was pretty near crying. I still see her...on the rocks."

But Lockie hauled ashore what was left of the *Pat and Jo-Anne*, bought some lumber, and hammered a new boat out of her that was out fishing again in six weeks. In 1968 he sailed around to Prince Edward Island and sold her. The bigger *Elaine and Sisters*, which'll go nine knots, he bought second-hand for $7,000.

Times are not too bad now. Half the kids are grown up, and the fish are biting. Last summer was Lockie's best. One day he brought in 14,000 pounds of mixed fish—the largest catch of his life—and he had many days when he came home from trawling with 12,000 or 13,000 pounds of fish. His average yearly income is now around $6,000 with about $2,700 taken off for operating expenses.

"I never got no help from nobody," he told me. "I did it myself. No one ever signed a note for me and I never had to mortgage the house. I was like *Mission: Impossible*. Never ran a grocery bill in my life."

He throws the dressed fish in a pail of sea water to clean out. He'll salt them later. We get in his '64 Ford and head home for dinner.

"The only thing I would've liked different in my life," he tells me on the way, "would have been enough money to buy an airplane. I like to go fast in a car when I'm by myself, and I'd like to fly. Plane is same as a boat, you know—you see nothing but sky, or you see nothing but water and sky....Yeah, I would've liked to have been a pilot."

I sit in the shed watching Lockie building lobster traps. We had fried swordfish for dinner. On previous days we had fried mackerel, scallop chowder, tuna. It's all part of finding out about a fisherman's life—but I wish I *liked* fish.

Mac and Gordon are with us. Mac is helping his father, and young Gordon is keeping count of the notes I'm making. Mac plans to be "a hockey player or something" when he grows up; Gordon, "probably a grease monkey." Older brother Patrick studies electronics at a trade school in Halifax.

"Boys stayed fishing in the old days," says Lockie, "because there was no education. There's more of that now. They even get paid for going to school. Pat makes around $80 a week—as much as he'd make fishing."

The rain drums away at the plastic window covering, the radio is set at country music, there's the smell of tar rope. Lockie hammers and sweats but the work is going well and over the noise this long afternoon I learn the following:

- Take three sills, four oak slats, three steamed oak or spruce boughs, 30 lathes, 110-pound test thread, two "kitchen beads," two maple rings, four flat ballast rocks, hard-test nylon line, a few bits of rope, and one pound of nails. Put it all together, and you've got a lobster trap. It takes Lockie an hour and a half to build one. The cost of material is $7.

- He has gone to see one movie in 14 years. It starred John Wayne.

- All year round, he fishes for halibut, haddock, codfish, mackerel, swordfish, herring, lobster, cusk, and so on. But what Lockie likes doing more than anything else in the world is going up a river and fishing for trout. He'll stay out three days.

- One thing he's looking forward to, "after all the kids are reared up," is taking Irene and going up the St Lawrence Seaway in a boat.

- "Fish aren't born to feel sorry for. Fish are born for fishermen to catch and eat."

- He drinks dark rum.

- In winter, he and Irene sometimes go to card parties on Saturday nights, sometimes to bingo games. On Friday night when the stores stay open until 9 PM, the family drives to Liverpool for shopping.

- He has had three breakdowns at sea when the search and rescue people had to go out looking for him. He fell overboard once. It was January. His clothes froze to his body and his hair froze to his head, but he got out in time.

- He's never worn a lifejacket in his life. "I've no fear of the water. It doesn't matter if I'm one mile out or 40."

- He can swim.

- Sometimes coming in from lobstering, he'll boil lobsters in sea water: it's the only way, and he and the others on board will eat them, maybe with a bottle of sherry.

- Last winter Lockie and Mac caught six rabbits with their own snares. Irene cooked them but she didn't eat them because they looked too much like cats.

- Lockie's only advice to his oldest son was: "You must decide yourself what you want to do with your life."

- Lockie's advice to Canada: "Well...keep the ball rolling, I guess."

- The only time he gets homesick on board is on a fine, moonlit night. "You really miss a woman on a boat then."

   Lockie is United Methodist. He used to go to church a lot, but he doesn't any more. "All they preach about is fellas drinking. They don't preach about the Bible. They quit preaching right, so I quit going. The only place you can hear a good sermon these days is on the radio.

   "I think about God all the time, whether I go to church or not. I think about Him on the water. It's somebody pretty powerful who made this world. On board when I go to sleep I say a little prayer like: 'Thank you dear Father that I am alive and I hope to be alive tomorrow. Amen.' I never had much trouble finding the trawl next morning."

After supper we sit in the living room and watch TV. The most striking object is a huge bouquet of plastic pink roses on the television set. Two rifles and a glued-together jigsaw puzzle of a Rhineland scene hang on the walls. Chairs and couches are covered with blankets so you can put your feet up.

Irene and Lockie and I move to the kitchen for a rum. Clothes hang drying by the stove. It smells of the bread Irene baked earlier. Lockie takes a pan of hot water from the stove and has a shave over the sink.

We talk about good moments. And one of the best was when Lockie finished wiring up the house, 16 years ago, and they got lights for the first time.

"She just went around switching switches," he recalls.

They never did get a phone in, though they've talked about it.

The arrivals of each of the kids were happy occasions, of course. Most of them were born at home.

"I brought one of 'em, you know," Lockie says. "Doctor didn't get here in time, nor a woman, so I did it myself. *That* was a good moment."

I'd asked Lockie before why he was a fisherman, and he had answered, but I felt not completely enough. Now I ask it again and he answers in much the same words:

"It's the being free. Doing whatever you want to do. You get up in the night and you don't feel good—you don't go out. You go back to bed. But if you do feel good, well, you go out fishing. If you've got a steady job you *have* to get up and be there *every* morning....It's the being free, I guess."

Later, making my way with a flashlight through the wet grass to the outhouse, I think that maybe that *is* all there's to it.

Next afternoon I leave. Lockie and Irene drive me to Liverpool.

She's turned unbelievably mild, there's no wind, the sun moves in a cloudless sky. From the highway we can see the *Elaine and Sisters* in the blue water by the causeway. I ask Lockie to stop. I'd like a last look. When I get back in he doesn't start the car immediately.

"I'd like to get away from the sea when I knock off," he says. "Way back on a farm somewhere. Then I wouldn't have to think about the water."

Then, staring pensively over the bay, "One day she's rough, the other day she's as smooth as a lake. That's the...the miracle of the ocean, I guess."

And he starts the car.

Chapter 10

"The Mountain Belongs to the Bums"

The snow fell slow and straight as it had all evening. It was about 11 PM. If you stood still and didn't breathe, the silence was total. Yet hard rock was blasting in the house only a dozen yards away. A few steps further, towards a frozen lake, and you couldn't see the house any more. A ramshackle structure by the railroad tracks in Alta Lake, 71 miles northeast of Vancouver, it had been crowded and hot and held too many different kinds of smoke, including that of the wood-burning stove.

The people inside the house had been jubilant when it started to snow.

"The Man is laying down a great boogie carpet for us," one had said. The "for us" is important. There was no question but that the snow was theirs. So, also, the land where it settled. A few minutes down the highway there rose a magnificent mountain—Whistler, 7,118 feet—and they believed they owned that, too.

"The mountain is ours," one had said during supper (moose steak, homemade beer, and apple pie). "The weekenders, they never get it. Not even the people who save all year to come up for two weeks. We're on it *all the time*. We're the only ones who really know it; and it knows us. The mountain belongs to the bums."

His word, not mine. To be specific: ski bums—men and women who *live* to ski. That old house was loaded with them that night [1973]. The ones who cut the snow first. The ones who every weekday, all winter long, weather permitting, are on their boards whispering, thudding, chattering, and scraping down the mountain, tracking the deep powder, taking runs where no one else dares, plunging into unexplored creek beds, shooting off cornices, their adrenalin rushing like crazy. "Getting it together on the mountain," is what dominates their life and determines their style. It isn't a common motivation, nor readily understood. Photographer Toby Rankin and I had roamed the Whistler area for four days asking ski bums about it. A long-time skier himself, Rankin already knew, actually. But I've never skied, and the joy, the mystique and fascination of it were foreign; and were largely still so on that fourth and last night....

We connected with the bums—only a few: they're always skiing and hard to pin down—in bars, shacks buried in snow, and on the mountain. They said there were about 50 of them around, meaning the people who contrived to do the maximum amount of skiing at a minimum cost. There were many around Whistler—hotel and lodge employees, for example—who *worked* to ski. And there were those who were simply rich enough to stay up the whole season. But the bums worked as little as possible—it interferes with skiing—and didn't have private incomes. Tough and ingenious survivors, they were outsiders who came into their own only on the mountain. The straight folk didn't care for them much.

"Down there in Soo Valley it's nothing but orgies," said a bartender. "All the time!"

Soo Valley was a few miles up the highway towards Pemberton. There, on the edge of a lake, spectacular mountains all around, 12 small cabins are nestled in the snow. Once it had been a milling site. Now some 20 ski bums live there. They rent the cabins from a land development agency for $75 a month. There is no electricity and no running water. They had winterized the buildings themselves.

It was night when we visited. A lot of dogs started barking. Weak, orange light winked through the trees.

Al Davies lived in the first cabin. He was reading *Bury My Heart at Wounded Knee* by Dee Brown, and wasn't in the least surprised to see us. He wore patched, shiny jeans and a shapeless sweater. He was lean and hawk-nosed, his grey hair grew towards his shoulders, and a moustache covered most of his mouth. We had brought a bottle of wine, but Al had no corkscrew and just pushed the cork inside. His place was cluttered, and lit by a solitary oil lamp that smoked. A wood stove hummed and snapped.

Al said that he was 45 years old.

"I guess I'm the oldest ski bum around here." One of his two adult daughters was in the last month of pregnancy. "A gramps any day," he said, "and I don't even know what I'm going to be when I grow up."

Born in Montreal and raised in Vancouver, Al learned to ski at ten and has since stayed close to the mountains. He said he earned his living variously as a newspaper reporter, commercial artist, piano mover, insurance salesman, truck driver, and sign painter. He had served one year of military duty in Korea.

"When I got out, I couldn't get back to the mountains fast enough."

Hollyburn, Grouse, Apex, Big White, Silver Star, Todd, Mount Seymour, Steven's Pass—Al has lived near and skied them all. But Whistler was the best—"If the snow's good you can ski down seven miles nonstop." For Al, now, life couldn't be better.

"I learn about myself on the mountain," he said. "When I've made a good run, I know it. You look back up at the tracks and you've made a statement. All you want to do is do it again.

"The adrenalin rush you get ups your strength and it can stay with you for hours. You'll never hit a tree, and if you do it's the tree that'll fall. I've come off the mountain and not been able to sleep till 3.

"Then there are the memory days when you're doing it all over again. Eyelid movies.

"Love for the sport just doesn't diminish. And what do other people say? They don't put me down. They say, 'Gee you're lucky. I wish I could do it.' And I say, 'Well, get it together. Do it!'"

Al's enthusiasm was making him sweat. There was, he said, only one thing missing.

"I've never spent a winter without an old lady. A good old lady is hard to find, but there's always an old lady. Trouble is you may have to teach her to ski. Teaching your old lady to ski is like teaching her to drive...and it interferes with your skiing."

Nothing disturbed the stillness behind the house by the tracks. Al, I realized, had not just been the first but also the most talkative ski bum encountered. The others, all of them in their 20s, had shown a mixture of disinterest and mild distrust, or simply hadn't been very articulate. Still, I had gathered that Al's way of life was roughly the same as theirs. Work a little in the summer and fall at lumbering or construction, and save your money. The first and absolutely essential expenditure is the $155 season ski tow pass. (Equipment and clothing manufacturers often give them merchandise for testing.) In winter, accept occasional short-term jobs—not when the skiing is good, of course—and live off savings and unemployment. Interesting, too, how many weekenders will stand you a meal or a drink. Transportation is rarely a problem with so many other people with cars around.

Al's living expenses consist of about $9 a month for rent and $60 for food, smokes, etc. Socks and underwear he washes himself in an old copper tub. Other laundry regularly finds its way to the Laundromat 18 miles away in Pemberton.

Al supplements his income by selling T-shirts that say things like, "Don't Trust Anybody Under 6,000 Feet," and "U.I.C. Ski Team." He is never without a backpack full of them.

Al said he didn't see his future changing much—unless the mountain got too crowded. The fewer people on it the better the ski bums like it. They rarely go up on weekends. The "turkeys" from the city, they say, stand in herds around the chair lift then going gabble, gabble, gabble. No—Saturdays and Sundays were to smoke a little, drink a little, and check out new chicks.

"So many people do jobs they hate," said Al. "That's no way to live! The weekender—he only lives two days a week. To keep what I have now I'm prepared to do anything—carpentry, pipefitting. I adjust easily. I know I'll always get it together, get the bread. There's nothing humiliating about asking for work.

"You rediscover things here. Baking bread, chopping wood, on a crisp morning going down to the creek for water. You really notice seasons change—suddenly the river is flowing faster. It's all part of the life. A voyage of discovery."

Thus Al Davies. And thus, too, the others as we met them.

René Paquette from Ville St Laurent, Quebec, was lying on his bunk listening to music. The bunk was built high off the floor for more heat. The Cassette worked on a 12-volt car battery. Into his third year at Whistler, René was apparently one of the best skiers around. A bearded, pink-faced blonde man, he said it was easy to feel but hard to talk about the joy of skiing. Yet words flowed fast when he tried.

"You get addicted. You become part of the mountain. You get an attachment for it. The more you do the better you get. Finally, it's so simple it's like walking down the street. You carve it down and you're just altogether. Friends share their energies on the mountain. It's total freedom. Purity.

"I know I'll be into it all my life. I don't worry about tomorrow. Now matters. I ski, I eat good, there's booze, there are women.

"I'm very aware of what I look like skiing. The rush is to have people smile all day long. That's my goal, man: keep smiles on people's faces. They don't know what we're doing and they want to know....It's like a white carpet, man. It sparkles. And then you're into it. It's so soft, so soft, so soft...and you're so stoned...and you keep going. Oh man...!"

Paul Matthews from Seattle was in the Roundhouse on top of Whistler for a fast coffee. It was cold and there was a raw wind, but he was anxious to get going. The most athletic looking of the ski bums, he was slim, wide-shouldered, and wore his hair surprisingly short. He, too, lived in Soo Valley.

"There aren't many things you can do that are as happy and intense as skiing," he said. "It's eyeball to eyeball with nature, a series of moments of truth. Sometimes it's better than sex.

"Vancouver's mothers don't like their daughters to come skiing at Whistler. Because if they meet us bums...they might disappear and not be heard from till spring."

And thus there were Lyle Featheringstonelough from Vancouver, John Heatherington from Toronto, Joyce Neilson from San Francisco, Lynda Brady from Vancouver and her "old man" Bruce Prentice from Winnipeg. And others, but introductions weren't always part of the scene.

Bruce and Lynda hosted the meal of moose on the last night. They shared the old house by the track with three others. By coincidence, all those mentioned were there, as well as a number of nameless ones. Friendly, healthy-looking people, with glowing cheeks, good teeth, and bright eyes. Occasionally, the eyes might be a bit off, less alert, turned inward a little.

It was a good evening. At some point somebody said we should see *The Worst Ski Movie in the World.* Homemade, it was, of course, all about skiing on Whistler. The title was not inappropriate. They turned the volume up on the record player and rock music slammed around the room. Most of them must have seen the film a dozen times, but whenever their beloved mountain showed its face it was greeted with loud "right ons" and "far outs."

At various times, René, Paul, and others had stressed that their involvement with skiing was not an "ego trip." During a quiet moment after the film, hostess Lynda, who has skied BC's mountains as much as most, contradicted this.

"A lot of people are so lonely," she said, "and skiing is the only thing they have. It's one big ego trip."

The talk that entire evening was about skiing. If other topics surfaced, it was never for long. Hour after hour it went and most of it, needless to say, was beyond me. Later though, in the silence outside, I remembered a bit of conversation between Al and Lynda. It was about cross-country skiing.

Lynda: "I went for the first time the other day. Fantastic! I was getting back to the source!"

Al: "Fast skiing is working the motor. Cross-country is a different pace—mellow. You can't see much going fast. Cross-country you really see the land. Time seems to go at a different rate. It will even just stand still...."

I had been in that dark, absolute stillness for a while, and I thought I understood a little of what they meant.

When I got back, somebody said we should troop up to one of the lodges for a drink. Lynda and Bruce said no. They were going cross-country, a few hours into the snow and on to that dark lake. The big group left by the front door, loud and throwing snowballs, Lynda and Bruce by the back door. Those two probably never said a word till they got home again.

In the bar, our company of 12 or so settled in a circle in a corner. The place was packed. People laughed a lot and shouted to friends. The waiter came and took the orders. Most asked for Canadian beer, two asked for imports. The waiter returned and emptied his tray. They all looked happy. They owned the snow and they owned the mountain, and there was no question who was going to pay for the beer.

Chapter 11

"There's a Deep Hunger Today for the Simple Word of God"

The house grew still. Most of the singing and praying done, it was time for preaching. That's why, after all, folks had come to Ottawa's National Arts Centre that night [1971]. Some from hundreds of miles away. This old-time, Holy-Ghost, God-fearing, spirit-filled, soul-saving rally should now get down to *business*; it was time for the preacher. And he didn't make 'em wait—or only a *second*—and then he was up there, tall and handsome, striding across the vast stage, smiling into the lights. Rex Humbard: king of soul savers.

But before preaching, before telling about the "three dimensions," before letting that powerful voice really go, Humbard wanted the folks to meet the others on stage: wife Maude Aimee, sons Rex Junior and Don, sister Leona and husband Reverend Wayne Jones, brother-in-law Reverend Charles Jones from Texas, the singers, the musicians, and—"This *Weekend Magazine* fella who's bin travellin' with us!"

Mild applause.

"How many of ya *read* it?"

A nice show of hands.

"I hope he writes real *good!*"

Solid applause.

"I want ya," said the preacher, "to pray with me this man'll tell the truth about us!" And warmly: "But he will. He's that kind of fella!"

So be it.

Alpha Emmanuel Rex Humbard, 51, is pastor of two congregations. One numbers about 2,800 families, members of his Cathedral of Tomorrow in Akron, Ohio. The other, his "television ministry," spans the continent. It claims to be the largest congregation in the world. On Sundays, Humbard holds an hour-long, interdenominational service in his church, which is videotaped and distributed for broadcasting 14 days later to, at last count, 215 American and some 100 Canadian television outlets. Its audience is about the size of Canada's population, or more than 21 million. At year's end, Humbard told me, it will be on 400 outlets with an audience of at least 23 million.

"We won't *want* any more stations then," he said in his strong Arkansas twang, "cause we'll just be duplicatin' ourselves."

It's staggering exposure, the largest in television history. And as it's the viewers who pay for most of that exposure, it's clear many millions of Canadians and Americans believe in Rex Humbard.

I saw some of these people recently. After Humbard preached, after he "called them to the Lord," after he prayed with them, they swarmed by the hundreds around him to shake his hand. Many cried, many smiled, many did both, and some trembled. All looked hard into his eyes:

"Thank you, Rex!"

"I pray for you, Rex!"

"Fight the fight, Rex!"

"God's with you, Rex!"

"Watch you *every* Sunday, Rex!"

"God bless you, Rex!"

And Humbard pressed their flesh tirelessly, "Bless ya! Pray for me—I'll pray for *you!*" He shook *every* hand; was always last to leave a service.

Once a month Humbard and his TV regulars go on the road for a week of one-night rallies somewhere in the US or Canada. "We must meet the people," he says. Recently they flew into Ontario—Chatham-Peterborough-Orillia-Kingston-Ottawa. I joined them in Orillia, and went along to Kingston and Ottawa. And a friendly, hospitable group they were.

Attractive people. They really stood out that night among the crowd of 3,800 packed into Orillia's hockey arena. Well-fed, alert and sure, all 18 of them. Dressed in smart, stylish clothes, and polished boots, with ornate hairdos for the women and, for at least three of the men, toupees. Humbard looked fit and tanned, hair brushed and sprayed to perfection. He wore a black suit, pink shirt and tie, and black boots with a zipper up the side. Just before the rally he wandered around shaking hands with local notables. He had the glow people have when they are the centre of attention. Presumably it's like that with him all the time. There was no doubt he was the star.

The police chief said it was a record crowd. There were folks in wheelchairs and on crutches, and one man on a stretcher under a red blanket. Folks of all ages, but mostly elderly and middle-aged. Some had brought their babies. There may have been some rich folks; there were certainly a lot of poor folks. Many of the women wore hats and most men were clean-shaven.

The mood was good in that big, ill-lit place. Hot dogs and chips and soft drinks were selling well. It was a night out. Not a fun night exactly, but not sombre either. How could it be with those beautiful, colourful people up on stage there, singing now, making music, talking and praying with those rich, twanging voices? And making little jokes, like Wayne Jones, associate pastor, asking for a show of hands to see how many thought there would be an offering tonight. Lots of hands went up of course. And that "card" brother Wayne said:

"Well, we won't disappoint ya!"

And it moved so quickly and smoothly. Song into talk into selling records into song into a short prayer into song....And people smiled listening. "Put your Hand in the Hand of the Man from Galilee," "Take Me to Calvary," "Reach Out to Jesus," "How Great Thou Art."

And then Rex. So sure up there. *Positive.*

"Lord, touch your servant tonight. Let this not be a message of Rex Humbard but a message of God, because the Spirit of God rests upon the words. Give an ear to hear, a mind to believe, and a heart to receive....Amen."

And he was off and running. Lord, what a salesman! What a salesman of the Lord! Short, vivid words rang through the place, running one after the other, hammering home the simple message, or so the message sounded—Seek the Saviour! Repent! Be born again! One illustration linked to the next, each a jewel of common sense, unarguable. He paced the stage, microphone in left hand, the right chopping, waving, fluttering, grasping, and pointing. Now and then, he asked for a show of hands to see if folks agreed. And hands went up fast. Once he called for an "old-fashioned Amen." And everybody went "Amen." Mental and physical man were doing fine, he said, but spiritual man was not. That was our third dimension and we were neglecting it. The little words ran on, pouring forth with hardly a pause, sometimes rising to a pitch like a slap and then diving low to husky pleading. Up and down, fast to slow to fast, a rhythm working, *connecting* all the little words, opening a path that looked so good to walk, showing light that seemed so warm, creating a mood of ease...maybe.

"Have ya bin born agin? I ask ya, have ya bin born agin? Is the Spirit of God within ya? Do ya understand spiritual things? Do ya love the Kingdom of God? The Word of God? The Things of God? The Commandments of God? If you *do*—it's 'cause you've bin born agin and ya love the things God wants ya to love....Ya see things the world don't see, ya understand things the world don't understand—because ya're s-p-i-r-i-t-u-a-l!"

And very softly: "And everyone that's had that experience in this room knows what I'm talkin' about. And everyone that doesn't, doesn't know what I'm talkin' about."

The preacher as artist.

Finally, "altar call." And, as you see on television, folks shuffled to the front. Many wept. That night 287 joined Humbard in prayer. He was on stage on one knee with his eyes squeezed shut.

After final benediction from brother Wayne, many more came forward, now to shake Humbard's hand. The mayor came up, a federal MP, and a Jehovah Witness of immense fortitude. To the famous preacher standing knee-deep in converts, he handed a little book, saying earnestly, "I think you should read this."

"Thank ya, friend," said Humbard. "Bless ya!"

When the last well-wisher had gone, we piled into rented cars and made for the nearest pizza place. A lot of eating is done on the road. But with driving, flying, singing, and preaching, they burn it up. Rex Junior, 27, reportedly eats five full meals a day.

Lots of people dropped by the table to bless the star.

"See you Sunday, Rex!" said a little girl smelling of chewing gum.

Humbard said he "preached hard" that night. He ordered pizza and spaghetti with meat sauce and talked: "People watch us 'cause of the message. They're *lookin'* for somethin'. I'm down to earth. Got a problem, man? The Lord is interested in it. I want to pray for ya! The Lord can meet your need! *This* is it! It's giving the people what they *want.* I believe the Bible is the Word of God. I don't understand all of it—but I believe it.

"Three weeks ago a man and his wife came up to me in Flint, Michigan. Big fella. He says, 'Remember bein' around here three years ago, Rex?' I says, 'Yeah.' Man says, 'I came down front that night. I was one of the worst alcoholics in Michigan. I was rough. I beat my wife. You ask her. I was unkind to my kids. I cursed. I gambled. But after comin' down that night I haven't drunk a drop. You ask my wife!' And his wife, she was cryin'.

"In a few weeks we're flying to Israel to do a TV special. I'm charterin' a 707 jet and I'm doin' somethin' that's never bin done before—having a communion service five miles high! I'm having this man in Bethlehem make these little-bitty communion cups out of olive wood so every one on that plane who takes communion gits to keep that cup.

"I don't git into issues. Never. I leave that to the politicians, to the military men.

"They're trying out my progr'm in Tokyo, in Mexico City, in Manila."

And next morning driving to the airfield near Peterborough where their Viscount waited to fly them to Trenton, Humbard talked: "Couple of years ago we had a rally 'round here, and this 80-year-old lady from Belleville came up to me and said, 'Rex, it was seeing you or the hockey game, and you won. Now all I want in life is to see you in the Cathedral of Tomorrow.'

"And then when Maude Aimee and I celebrated our 25th wedding anniversary in the church, in comes this little old lady in her wheelchair. 'Now I've seen the Cathedral and I can die happy!' she said. 'Don't you do that now!' I said."

Vivacious and outspoken, Maude Aimee said that the week before they'd been down in Nashville cutting records; that the next time she was in Montreal she'd like to stay in the Chateau Champlain; that Humbard's greatest asset was his photographic memory; and that you can tell people's characters by the condition of their shoes.

And Rex said: "All the rallies are the same. People are the same. Their problems are the same. And in every block in every city people have those problems. I fly over 'em and look down and I say every one of those homes is a p'tential pulpit. Years ago I tried to git into St Louis. I tried and tried to break that market but they wouldn't sell us TV time. One night I was flyin' home over St Louis and I'm lookin' down and seein' all those lights and in this plane I begin to weep. What an area! And I cain't git the Gospel into those homes! So I sent my man back the next day and this time he gits a good answer. Now when I fly over St Louis I say every one of those homes is a p'tential pulpit!"

The troupe carries its own sound equipment—4,000 pounds of it—and everyone helped load it into the plane, including a young photographer from the ad agency Humbard's corporation owns. Before we took off, Rex prayed for a safe trip to Trenton.

A rented truck and four cars waited at the air base. While the equipment was being unloaded the preacher and his two sons wandered the field with an air-force man pricing planes. They particularly liked an enormous military freighter. A big truck was just coming out of it.

"When Vietnam eases up," said Rex Junior, thoughtfully, "there should be a surplus of those planes."

Son Don, 23, said they could get a Mercedes truck and just pile all the stuff in and drive it into the plane. Much simpler.

"That'd be a blast," he said.

Then a Britannia landed and their interest shifted.

"Welcome Rex Humbard," said the sign outside the hotel in Kingston.

"That's *nice*," said Rex Humbard.

While the equipment was being set up at Kingston Memorial Centre that afternoon, Rex Junior explained that he produces and directs the television show and is in charge of logistics on the road. Brother Don is technical director. There are a younger brother and sister home in Akron.

"Dad's one of the most fascinating men I've ever come across," Rex Junior told me. "And I've met some fascinating ones...Jimmy Hoffa, men of that calibre. When Dad jumps off that stage to shake hands, that's his kicks. That's no show—that's his kicks."

Humbard's own words had been: "It feeds my heart."

"Dad's also got a very good, quick business mind," Rex Junior said. "A lot of people are fooled by him. Another thing is his naiveness. People tell shady jokes and he genuinely doesn't get 'em. I guess the TV ministry would die, if Dad died."

About his work, Rex Junior said: "We've created a personality. A pretty good-sized personality. What we're doing is as exciting as I could do on any other TV show."

And he talked a little about data processing, equipment purchases, new personnel, flight operations, publicity, executive committees, policy decisions, until it was time to get ready for the rally.

Humbard came in a bit later, splendidly dressed, exuding energy. He stopped and fingered my shirt. "I *like* that," he said and moved on to shake hands with local notables.

The rally went as well as in Orillia and as well as the one the next night in Ottawa. As Humbard said, the rallies were much the same. The revival troupe people were professionals; each item on the program connected nicely with the next. Still, Kingston was a bit different. I need not, perhaps, have gone on to Ottawa next day. But then I would have missed a luncheon for Humbard with some MPs and a senator. It was hosted by Robert Thompson (PC—Red Deer) who introduced his friend as "the man who is making the greatest impact for Christianity in Canada today." And Humbard told the politicians: "There's a deep hunger today for the simple Word of God. It's greater than I've seen in 38 years in the Gospel."

But Kingston. The place was jammed and at the "invitation" 309 came forward. Afterwards Humbard jumped down and shook hands. Hundreds were around him. I stayed close. So did Humbard's photographer.

A thin man in his late 40s rolled up in a wheelchair. Humbard gripped his shoulder and said, "God Bless ya!" The man said, "Thanks, Rex." Then he wheeled around the preacher but stopped in front of me.

"Listen," he said, and went on before I could say I wasn't with the group. "I'm a paraplegic. But I also have this bladder problem. Doctor told me to drink liquids. Water, juice...and beer. Now you tell me—is drinking beer a sin?" He looked up then. His face was wet from crying.

"I'm not...." I started. "If your doctor...."

But he wanted an answer.

"Guaranteed *not* a sin!" I said.

"Thanks!" said the man and wheeled away.

I shivered.

Humbard was shaking hands with a young man with dark curly hair. The young man kept saying, "Thank you! Thank you!"

I talked to him a moment later. He was trembling, breathing hard, and his brown eyes were moving all over. He was 20 years old, he said, and his name was Gordon. He came from a village 12 miles away. He'd had almost no steady work for a year. He had $500 in savings in the bank, and tonight he had made out a cheque for $50.

"A lot of things built up in me," he said, gulping air. "There was a compulsion in my breast....I feel God in *here*," and he thumped his chest. "I've been watching Rex for a year. I knew I had to come tonight....I was a man off by myself, no friends...."

And the brown eyes kept moving.

Just then Humbard called over the heads of people for me to meet somebody.

She, too, was sitting in a wheelchair. She was very old and wore a wide-brimmed green hat.

"The lady from Belleville!" Humbard shouted.

She was holding one of his hands in both of hers, looking up at him. "I weep when you weep, Rex," she was saying, "I laugh when you laugh."

Humbard signalled the photographer. "Get a shot of this!" he said. Then he wheeled the old lady around so they faced the photographer. "Smile, ya hear," he said, smiling himself. "Keep praying for me now!"

Click went the camera.

To Spread the Word: A Cathedral, Two Planes, and a Girdle Company

Rex Humbard, 51, was born in Little Rock, Arkansas, the oldest of six. He came by his fundamentalism naturally: his parents, both evangelists, brought their children into religious work early. In *Put God on Main Street*, his autobiography, Humbard tells how the family grew up during the Depression, crisscrossing the continent singing and preaching the Gospel. "We were the poor folks poor folks called poor folks," he recalls. Eventually, things picked up when the Humbards acquired a tent—The Gospel Big Top—and broke into radio.

Humbard, a high-school graduate, has no formal religious training. He was ordained by his father.

In 1942, after the Sunday night service at Cadle Tabernacle in Indianapolis, Humbard married his beautiful Texan wife Maude Aimee Jones while 8,500 people looked on. (She sings solo on the program and is a star in her own right.)

The family was still travelling in 1952 when Humbard decided to settle in Akron, Ohio, because, "God had work for me there."

"He gave me an idea," the book says. It was to build a great church and bring the Gospel via television to all the United States and Canada. "I had $65 at the time," he says. Humbard has built the church, created the "television ministry" and, in the process, developed a multifaceted, multimillion-dollar, religion-business empire.

A few details:

- The nearly 5,000-seat Cathedral of Tomorrow in Akron is the largest interdenominational church in the world. It is a huge, domed, circular, glass-and-marble structure that cost $3.5 million. A special feature is a 100-by-50-foot cross suspended from the dome with 4,700 light bulbs that can be illuminated in 60 patterns of red, white, and blue.

- The operation's colour television equipment is estimated at over $2 million.

- Humbard said the television ministry is paid for by viewers' donations. This year's budget, he said, would be around $7 million.

- If viewers' "prayerful support" doesn't quite make it, the balance will come from Cathedral of Tomorrow Inc., he said, which has capital assets of more than $14 million.

- Humbard said the corporation owns an ad agency; a girdle-manufacturing company; an electronics company; a multimillion-dollar, fully equipped college; a 52-seat Viscount turboprop; and another smaller plane. The corporation is building a television station next to the church. This will include a 1,300-seat restaurant and a $4-million, 750-foot tower with a revolving dining lounge modelled after Calgary's Husky Oil Company tower.

- The organization's latest acquisition, purchased in June reportedly for $10 million, was a complex of new structures in downtown Akron, including a 24-storey office building, a 2,150-car parking lot, and a 14-storey motel.

- Humbard said Cathedral of Tomorrow Inc. is a non-profit corporation created to spread the Gospel. As president, he draws a salary of $500 a week.

- He said that, while corporate profits may go to help the television work, viewers' contributions are never used by the corporation. He said the operations are kept strictly separate, as is the church's own $500,000 budget. This also goes for his Canadian office in Toronto, which spends $60,000 a month on the cause, he said. "All the money taken in Canada," he told me, "must stay for our work there."

- The Humbard operation has a staff of about 200.

Chapter 12

"What Suffering and Death That Light Has Averted"

From a letter by a visitor to Cape Roseway on 3 April 1890.

For more than one hundred years that light has stood as a guide to the poor mariner. What a joy has entered the hearts of many a crew when darkness and storm prevailed and all depended on one sight of that grand old light which had safely guided thousands into one of the best harbours in the world. Oh, what suffering and death that light has averted in those long years....

What a weight of responsibility rests on the keepers of those stations—human life and property all depending upon the faithful keepers.

On the first day "she was fine," with sun, no clouds, and an April wind that bit only a little. In the small roofless rooms along the rocks it was warm and still, except for the sea's gossip below.

But during the night the gulls got busy. Barking in their high-pitched, furious way, they dragged in the fog. Thousands of them, each with a thread in its beak, pulled it from far out in the Atlantic and draped it around McNutt's Island. McNutt sits nine miles out of Shelburne on Nova Scotia's south shore. The fog shut out the mainland, the moon, the sound of the water, and finally the birds' own screams.

It even walled off McNutt from Cape Roseway, its most southerly point, where on a high cliff the lighthouse stands. And *there* it set off an automatic fog alarm. "Doooooooooaaaaaatttt!" It went at intervals timed to the second, sounding like a lonely, sick cow. "Take care!" was its message to the hardy men in little ships out on the deep water. It bawled on and on all of the second day and all of the third.

I listened in bed to the silences between the blasts until a grey dawn broke, bringing back the sounds of the sea and the crazy gulls, and then a light, steady rain....Like everything else on Cape Roseway, the sounds took on an easy rhythm. Today would be like yesterday and like tomorrow. I had witnessed no shipwrecks, no storms, and was pretty sure I wouldn't. I thought my visit was proving singularly uneventful, so I went back to sleep until Lyndon Crowell came in to get his sailboat.

Lyndon had every right to come in because it was his room. This was a Sunday [1972] and he was home for the weekend from school on shore. He's eight and the son of assistant lighthouse keeper Barry Crowell, 31, a small, neat man with a moustache, dreamy blue eyes, and many hobbies. His mother is pretty, dark-haired Donna who runs the cleanest home in Canada; there's also his sister, Annette, aged four.

Lyndon's parents provided board and room during my stay. All over their house hang Barry Crowell's paintings, most of them marine scenes. Barry, whose father ran a lighthouse, and who also has an uncle and a cousin in the business, has been at Cape Roseway nine years. He and Donna come from the nearby villages of Upper Port Latour and Baccaro.

Lyndon said he was going to take his boat out on the rocks. Some hollows there held water left by the last heavy seas. Day two had begun.

I did what I did most of the time on the island—I went visiting. I would sit around in Barry's home awhile, and then walk about 30 paces west into the house of Harry ("van") Buskirk, my official host and head lighthouse keeper, and there we'd chat (Van, who is 52, has 11 children and not much room to spare). For three days, back and forth, visiting.

It was past 10, so Van would have stood his watch and be having coffee. He has the 2 to 10 AM watch; Barry, 2 to 10 PM. There used to be a third man until semi-automation. Now there are two four-hour periods when the station is, in fact, unwatched.

Van's house was less tidy than Barry's. That was partially because of all those children, though two are married and "off," and two were away fishing on the west coast. It was also because Van's wife Ruth believes in cooking big meals and keeping everybody in clean clothes but, once that's done, she likes to pack a lunch and take off over the rocks with her youngsters or into the woods to the north.

As on the day before, when Van and I followed her among the spruce trees, along the trail lay stealthily dropped candies the kids would find coming back. In a small, windless space she and the children were running around barefoot. Ruth was perspiring. "You know," she puffed, "I've never sat around with a group of women having coffee or been to a cocktail party. Never *will* either!

"Salespeople don't come to my door. Not even the Avon lady!" she said on the way back "What I like best here is the privacy."

The van Buskirks have had that—on three different islands—all the 26 years of their marriage. In the old days there was no radiophone or electricity, and often they couldn't get off for as long as five weeks. Ruth was a Boston girl who came visiting Nova Scotia in summer; Van, a fisherman's son from Murphy Cove, about 50 miles northeast of Halifax.

One thing about the van Buskirk home, it was always bright inside despite fog and rain. There are lots of windows and Ruth never pulls the shades. "I like looking at the sky," she said.

Van was on the living room couch that morning, socked feet on a chair. His face and neck are tanned and seamed from outdoor living, his hands wide and strong. He still fits with ease into his wedding suit.

Ruth was baking bread in the kitchen. When everybody's home, she'll do three loaves and a pan of buns a day. (Donna, that day, baked two blueberry, one apple, and one lemon pie.) Ruth isn't a small woman, and she looks very fit. She practises yoga every day, and has large, very clear, grey-blue eyes.

Ruth brought in coffee and the makings for peanut-butter sandwiches on home-made bread. As always, she sat down next to Van and put her arm around him. Occasionally, I had to remind myself that these two had lived together for 26 years in very close circumstances and raised 11 children. Once they sat like that for nearly three hours. Maybe it's the island life that does it.

Talk went as easy as it had on the first day and as it would on the third. It was the same thing 30 paces east in the Crowell home. One subject led naturally into the next. Stories were told slowly with lots of details, opinions were expressed with care. There were no one-liners. It rained, so the children mostly stayed indoors and listened, or played Monopoly, or watched TV. There were small interruptions for cookies or coffee or orange pop. And conversation was helped, too, because by then I had already climbed the light-house to the top; touched the turning, warm light; walked the railed parapet in fear; inspected the new fog alarm and listened to the former one's voice—Van said the two sounded as different "as a big heavy fisherman and a little child"; studied the workings of the radio beam; looked at the machinery that kept it all going; understood that a lighthouse keeper is combination mechanic, electrician, carpenter, driver, sailor, plumber, ditch digger, painter, and boat builder; and roamed the mighty rocks below the light and saw them pounded by the sea.

None of which gave special insight into life at Cape Roseway, but it did make it slightly easier to understand what Van and Ruth and Barry and Donna were saying. Here is some of it.

Barry: "It'll take six months living here to appreciate what we're talking about."

Van: "If you like partying and that, this isn't the life for you. I like it because I feel free. Even in Shelburne I don't feel as free."

Donna: "It sometimes makes you cranky living on a place like this when it's foggy and raining. But I like the feeling of solitude."

Ruth: "I'd like to get off once every two weeks at most."

Barry: "I don't miss a damn thing here. What's there to do in town? Buy your groceries, do some errands, make your car payment, and come home...broke!"

Ruth: "The one big drawback to living here is having to board out the children on the mainland because of school. I find that very hard....I tried teaching them myself, with correspondence courses, but had to give it up."

Donna: "To get groceries you've first got to drive more than three miles to the wharf, cross with the boat, drive to Shelburne, load the groceries into the car, drive back, load 'em into the boat, cross to the wharf, lift 'em out, load the car, drive home—by then the groceries are all worn out!"

Van: "The sea, it's just fantastic! As much as I've been around the water, I still don't understand how fast she can change. From calm and smooth like now to beating those rocks—white and foaming as far as you can see."

Barry, on fishermen in a storm: "You know they're out there...you're *thinking* about them. But there's nothing you can do except keep this equipment going. That's the job. Sometimes you get a feeling you're worthwhile. All you can do when you see a boat floundering out there is stand and watch. Throw a rope to a guy to help him over the rocks? But what if it's night and winter...?"

Donna: "I'm always a bit scared in a boat. I don't really like boats."

Ruth: "The first, biggest, and best change was when electricity got to the station. The second was when we bought the freezer."

Van, on pollution: "I've got the whole sea, but here ordinary garbage is used for compost, cans go to the dump, and what's left is burnt. *Nothing* goes into that sea."

Van, on vacations: "I take them in winter and go lobstering. If I had the money and time maybe I'd see Newfoundland. But I'll probably never go....

"We were in Quebec two years ago. The Laurentians are pretty, but the island is prettier. I've got three sisters in Montreal. I can see them living there and wanting to come here. I *can't* see living here and wanting to go *there.*"

Barry: "I can sit and watch a storm for hours. I've lived with the sea all my life but, even so, every storm is different. I wouldn't want to live away from the ocean for long. I like its *sound.*"

Ruth: "This place is too lovely to keep to yourself. I wish I could find one mature adult to help me out and then I'd get about a dozen underprivileged children to come here in the summer."

Barry: "Two summers ago in July, which has 744 hours, we had 690 hours of steady fog."

Van: "In the old days we used to hand-crank the fog horn. The lantern, of course, was oil fed. And you were tied to the island because you were all alone: you always had to get back and get that light on."

Donna: "Sometimes I miss parties and things. Although we have company every weekend, it's a treat to get off now and then."

Barry and Donna told how Lyndon was almost born aboard an RCMP coast patroller at night during a storm with 40-knot winds. "The constables were more scared than I was," said Donna. They fought for hours to get her to Shelburne where she was raced to hospital under police escort.

Van and Ruth recalled the couple that ran Nicholl Island station, out of Ship Harbour east of Halifax. The man went gunning for ducks one stormy day in winter and told his wife that if he wasn't back by dark to turn the light on and come looking for him. He slipped on ice-covered rocks and shot himself in the stomach. Somehow he crawled to within 500 yards of the light. His wife and 11-year-old son found him in a pool of blood. She got the toboggan but he weighed some 250 pounds and couldn't be budged. They built a fire around him for warmth but he died in the night. Next morning she set out with the boy in a rowboat. She broke both oars on the ice, but finally managed to make it across.

Nicholl Island was the newly married van Buskirks' first posting. They moved in shortly after. The blood didn't seep into the ground till spring. The van Buskirks lived 13 years on Nicholl Island and remember it fondly. They raised sheep, ducks, hens, and a pig. A tame deer went swimming with them, and you could only coax it out of the house with oatmeal and molasses cookies.

On the third day, Barry and I took a walk over the rocks in the rain. Besides painting, Barry's interests include collecting rocks, driftwood, and guns; wine making; beachcombing (around the island once a week); cabinet making; wood carving; building models of wharves, lighthouses, boats, and fishing villages; and placing small signs around the place such as "Elephants Crossing" and "Lake Inferior."

The only ugly thing we saw was a huge ball of rusted barbed wire from the war days. On the way back Barry talked about his painting. On the first day, he had shrugged it off with, "You've got to do *something*." But he had more to say this time. Stopping at a great gully eaten away by the sea, he sat down on a boulder and looked at the water.

"I've done at least 12 paintings sitting here," he said. "And they're all different. A man could do a thousand paintings from right here. He needn't ever move."

I had a last coffee with the van Buskirks before leaving. We talked about all the good things you can do on McNutt Island. Sunbathe, swim, or walk *alone*, build tree houses, make little camps here and there, fish, visit gulls' nests in summer, pick four different kinds of berries, hunt ducks and deer, snare rabbits, bicycle, pick mussels, dig clams, ride a sleigh, row a dory, paint scallop shells, pick spruce gum for chewing, explore the beaches and woods, grow a garden, harness the dog to a toboggan, and so on.

"Oh yes, and in summer," said Ruth, "we sit on the lawn swing and sing 'Old van Buskirk had a light/And on that light he had a—' and we list everything we've got."

It's a long song.

And Then There Was Light

Alexander McNutt, an Irishman, reportedly attempted a settlement on the island in 1764. He called it New Jerusalem, and no cats were allowed because they weren't mentioned in the Bible. McNutt drowned in 1765 crossing to the shore. There is a cat on McNutt now and also a Sable Island pony, a dog, a lobster in an aquarium, a hamster, three tame rabbits and lots of wild ones, deer, squirrels, and all kinds of gulls and ducks. McNutt is four and a half miles long and two miles at its widest. There are, as well, two enormous, rusty, Second-World-War cannons set among the trees and pointing at the ocean.

Cape Roseway is the third oldest (1788) manned lighthouse station in Canada. It caters mostly to inshore fishermen and summer pleasure craft. The walls of the original building were made of locally found granite and plaster from burnt mussel shells. The first fog alarm was a cannon. Eventually it was discarded and flung down the rocks, but the current keepers restored it during Centennial year, and it stands guard by the flagpole. Fire destroyed the first lighthouse in 1959, so the Department of Transport built a new one 55 feet tall. Its top is blood red, like the roofs of the three homes and five sheds below, and its trunk is white. It looks built to last forever.

Cape Roseway's light is now semi-automatic, and its fog alarm entirely so; the latter reacts to a certain moisture content in the air. Men will soon no longer need to tend the equipment daily; it'll be done by remote control. There are some 300 manned stations in Canada and the government, in a program started this year, plans to have them automated by 1977.

So visit a lighthouse soon, if you want somebody to show you around. In the near future you'll find the wind and ghostly buildings where only ticking gadgets live. Lighthouse keepers will be no more.

Chapter 13

"A 'Good' Wolf Is a Dead Wolf"

My friend Michael and I got to Steve Everett's place around noon. It's a dilapidated summer cottage (Steve doesn't live there) on an inlet from Lake of the Woods just outside Kenora, Ontario, 120 miles east of Winnipeg. Steve, 63, is the best wolf hunter around these parts. Last year [1970], he was Ontario champion—he and his friend Jim Morgan, 36, killed 49. They did their hunting from a plane. Steve, a pilot during World War II, does the flying and Jim the shooting, but occasionally Steve likes to do some shooting, too.

Fifty yards below Steve's place, his two-seater aircraft on skis was parked on the frozen water, a tarpaulin covering its engine. Just by the front steps of the cottage lay four skinned wolf carcasses, stuck together in the cold, without heads, tails, or paws. Scattered on the floor of the unheated porch were 12 stiff wolf skins, clots of blackened blood still on the fur.

Inside there was a musty smell. Two dead wolves lay between some old chesterfields and chairs, thawing out. There was a fridge that didn't work, an empty soft-drink machine, a short wave radio, a pair of snowshoes in the window. In a corner was a box full of empty bottles, mostly rum. Two rooms in the back were boarded up; only the main room was in use. An iron stove gave off a fierce heat.

Steve and Jim and two other men sat around a table playing cards and smoking. They looked fit in a ruddy, windburned way. Steve had met my friend before. He told Michael that, in the morning, Kenora's radio station, CJRL, had a phone-in show on wolf hunting—which was quite a coincidence—and that most of the people who called to say they were against it didn't know what they were talking about. The other three watched him as he spoke, not us.

Michael and I had heard a portion of the program on the car radio. I remember a woman telling the announcer, "Look, I wish people would kind of leave wolves alone."

"I would like them to see what a wolf does to a deer when it's still *alive*," Steve said. "It brings the deer down and just starts eating at its hind quarter right then. It's sickening!"

Steve said shortly after the show a local photographer had come down to take pictures of dead wolves. Steve had told him to get off the property or he'd break his camera. He said he wanted nothing to do with newspaper people because they sensationalized everything.

"If they ever stopped wolf hunting, I'd cut my throat," he said. "It's the only sport I enjoy in winter. That's about all I do is chase wolves. I'm more conservation-minded than *anybody*—but I'm a sportsman!"

I hadn't been introduced yet, which right then was probably just as well. Michael nodded at me, and we took our leave. Back in town, we visited some Ontario department of lands and forests people. From them, from literature we gathered, and from other wildlife experts, we learned some facts about the wolf that afternoon.

There's been a bounty on wolves in Ontario since 1793. It's $25. When a hunter brings one in, the government people slice a cross on its snout so he can't collect twice. Last year, in the 12,173 square miles that make up Kenora District, bounties were paid on 217 timber wolves and 35 brush wolves—140 of them killed from aircraft. Wolves will kill livestock. But we were told there wasn't much reason for killing wolves in northwestern Ontario, "Canada's wolf hunting capital," because there's little livestock around. If the bounty were cut off, it was supposed, there would probably be less wolf killing. But wolves killed too many deer and moose; that is, hunters, resort owners, and outfitters *said* they did. These were the people, we learned, who do most of the pressuring for keeping the bounty. They want, in other words, more wolves killed so *men* can kill more deer and moose. But this didn't make sense when it was explained that the animal's competence as a killer is much exaggerated: for every ten to 12 tries, a wolf makes only one kill.

It seemed then that there was no valid reason for killing wolves at all, anywhere, except where they do damage to a farm or ranch. Nevertheless, by trapping, snaring, shooting, poisoning, and "expanding our development activities," we had managed in Canada to kill off the Great Plains wolf of the southern prairies and the Newfoundland wolf, and had nearly done so with the Vancouver Island wolf.

In the US, incidentally, the wolf has all but vanished and is now classified as an endangered animal under federal legislation. Scandinavia, including Finland, reportedly has no more than 25 wolves. And in the USSR, so evidence shows, it's the government's official policy to exterminate the animal. In recent years as many as 8,000 men in 740 teams have been organized and sent out to kill wolves.

Wolves kill big game. A mature wolf eats ten to 12 pounds a day if the hunting is good. But it kills to eat, and, when it's through, little is left but bits of fur and blood stains. Wanton killing, we were told, is almost unheard of; and when it does happen, scientists usually trace it to an animal with rabies, which in itself is rare. Also, wolves usually kill the old or ill or very young—because they're easiest to catch—thus actually aiding the survival of a herd by culling undesirable individuals and stimulating reproduction.

One source claimed that more than half of the deer killed by wolves are older animals, whereas 90 percent of what men shoot are fawns and females. Ecologically, it seems wolves are necessary to their environment. It isn't, in nature, a matter of wolves or deer, but wolves *and* deer.

Finally, studies show that wolves have an intrinsic birth-control system which, while the mechanics of it are still unclear, sees to it that wolf populations remain stable.

But if all this is true, why is it that, until about 12 years ago, the only "studies" of wolves, except for two or three, were, concerned with methods of *killing* them?

The reply was *Little Red Riding Hood*: the Little Red Riding Hood Syndrome, a concoction of myths, legends, exaggerations, and lies about the Big Bad Wolf handed down from generation to generation! And it was still perpetuated today, we were told. And true, it was hard remembering ever hearing anything *good* about the wolf. A good wolf is a dead wolf. It's always wicked and dangerous—the universal symbol of evil.

So what we were being asked was to believe that all the wolf killing was, basically, because of a children's story and stories like it. It had to be, because we were told then that biologists working and living among wolves have never felt the need to carry a rifle. But the clincher came when Douglas H. Pimlott, a zoologist at the University of Toronto, and the foremost authority on wolves in the country, said that he considered studying wolves "one of the lowest-risk professions in the world." Dr Pimlott also said that there is *not one authenticated case of a wolf killing a human being in North America.*

That evening my friend Michael and I called Steve and asked him and Jim to come over for a drink and to talk about wolf hunting. And they did.

Steve said his basic reason for hunting wolves was "outwitting the smartest, shrewdest, most intelligent animal there is. It's very exciting when you see 'em down there." He said it certainly wasn't the money. After the $25 bounty he might get $50 for the fur. On the 49 he killed last year, he made no more than $300 or $400 after expenses.

Steve said another reason for hunting them was that there were too many around. Three years ago, he had helped make an estimate of wolves within a 60-mile radius of Kenora. The count was about 3,000. (A rough estimate for all of Canada, according to Dr Pimlott, is 15,000. The densest wolf population is in Ontario's Algonquin Park—10 to 12 per 100 square miles. An average density for the timber wolf is one per 100 square miles.)

"For me it's a sport, an entertainment," Jim said. "And with all that flying you really get to know the country."

Jim used a shotgun. The bullet from it contains 41 lead pellets. At 50 feet, for instance, the pellets move in a 30-inch circular spread. He said the hideless wolf carcasses that we had seen were bait. They would drop them in the middle of a frozen lake, the ravens would come to eat, and then the wolves, curious, might venture out onto the open ice. He and Steve usually cruised at about 80 mph, 700 or 800 feet up. They would slow down to around 45 mph and sometimes fly a foot or less above the ice when coming in for the kill. If wolves spotted the plane, they'd make for cover on the nearest shoreline. The pilot would follow them and the gunner would drop "cherry bombs" at the spot where they had disappeared. A cherry bomb was a sort of firecracker that gave off a terrific bang. You could only get them in the US, he said. The bombs would panic the wolves and they might run right into the open again.

Steve said the flying got "hair-brained" at times. (Apparently, at least one wolf-hunting plane a year crashes around Kenora.) Jim said his job had its difficulties, too. A cherry bomb went off in his lap once, and another time he shot the plane's propeller.

I asked the hunters what they thought of wolves.

"They're a menace," said Jim.

"I've no use for them," said Steve.

The morning of our second day was bad for hunting: visibility was practically zero. We found Steve skinning the two wolves that had been inside thawing. The stink on the front porch as he sliced the fur away grew unbearable.

A bit later, four American hunters landed their aircraft in front of Steve's place. At the end of the week, Kenora would have its annual three-day carnival. One of the events would be a fly-in of wolf hunters, many of them from the US. In other years, as many as 30 planes had shown up. The Americans were middle-aged and rugged-looking—a cattle buyer, a post-office worker, an electrician and a crop-dusting pilot. One of them said that, during the carnival, "you dance, drink beer, eat fish chowder, and shoot wolves." He said the guy who shot most got a trophy and $100. Steve won it last year.

By midday, the weather had lifted and the Americans and Steve and Jim got ready to go hunting. On their way to the planes they stopped at the pile of bloody corpses outside the front porch. One of them lifted a pawless leg and a puff of stink came up.

They moved down to the planes, laughing. They were in good spirits, comfortable in each other's company. The afternoon promised adventure. Then the three aircraft roared off across the ice and into the gray sky.

Jack Howard, 36, a pilot from Kenora, took me up in a two-seater later just so I could get a feel of what it was like to hunt from one.

In the air Jack yelled over his shoulder that he, personally, didn't like wolf hunting. "It's a waste. Steve's pretty good, but some of those Americans that come up…for every one they shoot they cripple three that go in the bush and die. I used to do it. But not any more."

We skimmed over lifeless white lakes and bushy islands. Then Jack pointed to the right and flipped the plane that way—four black spots moving single file two miles away.

"Wolves, maybe!" Jack yelled.

But they were deer. They saw us and started racing for a nearby island. But we were so much faster. When we swung by, skis sometimes rattling over ice ridges, they were less than 25 feet away. A reasonable shot would have gotten at least two. Twenty minutes later the same thing happened with eight deer. But we saw no wolves that day. And neither did the six hunters.

We got to Steve's place next morning just as he and Jim had come in and were cutting a dead wolf down from the plane. It dropped to the ice and its head came to rest on its front paws. It was a male, about three years old, and it had seven shots in it. It was still warm. It looked a lot like a German shepherd—long legs with big feet and a large bushy tail. Its colouring was cream and gray and black. I asked Jim how much he thought it weighed. A short, powerful man, he heaved the wolf chest high in one lift.

"At least 90," he said.

Then he spread his arms and the animal fell with a crack on the ice. It was the head that made the crack. Blood gushed from the mouth and the tongue flopped out. Jim then tied a rope around its neck and dragged it up to the cottage. They left a red trail.

Afterwards, Steve, Jim, Michael, and I sat in the heated room. Jim played solitaire, Steve smoked a small pipe.

"Wolves don't like to travel in the wind," Steve observed, "Even eight miles is too strong. If the wind is bad, I've seen the beggars lie up for ten to 12 days."

But there really wasn't much left to talk about. It was time to go.

Earlier that day Michael had asked whether I thought I had a story. I'd said, "Well, maybe...." I suspected this answer made him a bit anxious. After all, he had spent his own time doing some preliminary research on this story. A Winnipeg businessman, it was he, in fact, who had suggested *Weekend* come to Kenora. But I was troubled. True, I'd learned that shooting wolves from a moving vehicle didn't deserve to be called a sport. And true, I'd learned that almost all killing of wolves is a stupid, shameful business. But this, somehow, to me then, didn't make a magazine article yet.

We got up, and Steve rose to show Michael and me out. On the front porch lay the scattering of wolf skins. Not dead animals any more. Just skins, furs—and fur is beautiful.

"I have two little girls at home," Michael said to Steve. "They wear parkas, you know, with little hoods. They'd look nice trimmed with fur. How much do you want for one of those skins, Steve?"

And then I had a magazine article.

"Shivers Run Rampant Up and Down Spines"

A "howl-in" is where people and wolves do a little howling together. Ontario's Algonquin Park in one of the best places in the world to catch this "grand opera of primitive nature." Last year, some 3,500 people travelled there to hear timber wolves howling in response to human imitations or tape recordings of their call. The idea is to search for wolves by driving along the roads at night, stopping to howl and listen, then going to another spot and trying again. When a pack is located and starts to answer, apparently, "shivers run rampant up and down the spines of listeners." It's been said: "Only a mountain has lived long enough to listen objectively to the howl of a wolf."

It's presumably possible to organize howl-ins anywhere there are wolves.

A Wolf in the Family

A couple I know in San Francisco had a Canadian timber wolf at home for two years. I called and asked about it and couldn't get them off the phone.

Lykaina (Greek for she-wolf) joined the household—two adults, a small boy, a basset hound, and a Siamese cat living on a houseboat—when she was 18 days old, "Don't even try for a master-pet relationship," an expert warned. "A wolf isn't a pet. Accept her as an *equal* member of the family. Don't expect obedience." It was, apparently, the cat and the dog that gave the wolf most of her basic training.

She: "At first Lykaina was like any small child—into everything. She especially liked playing with *left* shoes, leaving me with a half dozen right ones."

He: "She was incredibly intelligent and rational, and playful. When she got older it was OK for us, for instance, to leave her on the boat all day. Then we'd come home and she'd be terribly glad to see us. But if we wanted to go out again later—no way! 'I've been alone all day and I've been good,' she'd show us. 'Don't you *dare* go out!'

"I carry my wallet in my back pocket. During dinner, Lykaina sometimes lifted it with her teeth without me feeling a thing. Then she'd post herself where I'd have to look at her, holding the wallet in her mouth and laughing like hell."

She: "The two of us took her and the hound in a Volkswagen across to Prince Edward Island and back. People everywhere were in terror of her. 'Is it vicious?' they'd always ask. But she never hurt a thing in her life."

He: "If we went into a restaurant at night and left her alone too long she'd pull and push the light switch on the dashboard to let us know."

She: "Or she'd pull up the lock button on the door with her teeth and push the handle down with her paw and come out."

He: "She liked to run. We'd let her out of the boat very late at night and she'd roam all over—but she always came home at dawn. She *knew* she shouldn't be out on her own when light came....She scared people, but people scared her."

She: "One day two years ago she didn't come back. The whole neighbourhood looked for her. We don't know what happened. Maybe she was shot, or stolen, or maybe a car hit her and she went off somewhere in the hills to die."

He: "We still miss her...."

Chapter 14

Printer's Ink Is in His Veins
and All Over His Shirt

Ron Newsom had yelled over the phone from Bashaw, Alberta: "It's half cleaned up here and I've got some time—be glad to see you!"

That was not the whole and absolute truth, though. He certainly did look glad that damp day in the fall of 1972 when I came to visit from Montreal, but you could hardly call the place clean. He shook hands with both his ink-smeared ones; his first words were, "How about a drink?"

The *Bashaw Star* on Bashaw Avenue was not half cleaned up, nor a quarter. Once a livery stable, the 24-by-50-foot building had had its last paint job seven years before. Dingy and crowded inside, smelling of oil and ink, it probably never would get cleaned up. The chaos reached almost to the ceiling: stacks of newspapers, tables loaded with type, piles of boxes and cans, and massive steel machines. Under 12 weak light bulbs, the machines clicked and hammered; beneath them shuddered the floor. You moved with breath sucked in and hands in pockets—whatever you touched gave off black.

As for time, well, Newsom made some for me, but he hardly seemed to have it to make. It's a myth that there's lots of time in small towns. There may be less commotion, but life can be as busy as in a city and perhaps it's more intense. There's the closer involvement with others, for instance. That, certainly, is the case with the *Star*'s 59-year-old owner-editor—involvement up to his eyebrows. He admits it.

"You're a key person in this job. It's hard to get time alone. I've got to be with people. I'm not happy if I'm not. I love people."

And that, by the way, is the feeling a lot of people seem to have about him. "Nice" is an overused word, but Newsom has to be one of the nicest men in the country. At his home is a cup, a special award he got in 1970 from the Canadian Community Newspapers Association. The inscription reads: "For dedication to the community in which he lives and the townspeople of Bashaw with whom he fellowships." A couple of months later, Bashawers gave him a plaque for "service and dedication to this community above and beyond the call of duty." But most telling, I thought, was what I heard about his friend and fishing partner, Dave Lofstrand. Dave, who is about Ron's age, is area manager of Calgary Power Ltd. For years, he's been coming in every Saturday to work a full shift on the linotype machines—"as a hobby." One day he told Ron:

"If you ever sell your linotypes, I'm going to buy one and put it in the garage. So that when you're dead, I can go there and set some lines and remember our times."

Newsom disappeared for a moment to the rear of the shop and came back with two small clouded glasses of rye. He set them down on a desk that held a portable typewriter, a scattering of bills, and one of those old press cameras. He is a stocky man with powerful forearms. There isn't a grey hair on his head, but a complex of wrinkles has set in at the sides of his eyes, and the eyes have pouches beneath them. He would be well cast as either a psychiatrist, a priest, or a bartender. He has a lot of ink and oil on him, even on his face. He wore a working man's boots and loud-coloured clothing. He is partial to colour, I later learned. Some threads hang from his trouser pockets; a steel ruler sticks out of one of them.

I wanted to find out about the life of a small-town weekly editor—there are about 725 of them in Canada—and Newsom began to talk. His brown eyes, though, seemed to swim away from what he was saying. The eyebrows would leap up and the eyes would roam to the ceiling. He might then, out of the blue, mutter things like, "Life is sweet....My wife has a sense of humour and it permeates the house." Or: "Every age has its own grace."

The *Star*, said Ron, has a press run of 1,150, and 970 paying subscribers (at $3 a year) including some in the United States,

England—and Libya. The paper covers Bashaw (population 788), 89 miles southeast of Edmonton, and 11 other farm communities nearby. It varies in size from four to eight pages. Counting commercial printing jobs, the shop turns over about $20,000 a year; Ron's income is around $6,500. The staff consists of his wife Myrtle, who does all the bookkeeping, two part-time workers, 15 district correspondents (paid ten cents an inch) and ten in town.

The eyebrows rose at that point: "I'm happy. Myrtle is happy. That's worth a lot more than bucks. You can't live in this kind of community and not love what you're doing. You're dead if you don't. In my case, it's meeting people. Of the 2,000 that live around here, I know at least 1,700 by name."

And that, of course, is what the *Star* is all about—people. Its pages are crammed with their names and what they've been up to: births, deaths, engagements, promotions, marriages, showers, fires, confirmations, anniversaries, visits, graduations, holidays; who turned "82 years young," who sold peanuts on Saturday, and who took off for the World Contact Lens Congress in Japan.

And it's people who make up Bashaw's more than 20 clubs and associations, and people who go to the dances, and attend the seven churches. People act and paint, and play billiards, badminton, hockey, and bingo. And people hunt, fish, golf, snowmobile, skate, and curl. And it's people who get into trouble.

"Court reporting I do mostly in the abstract," Ron said. "No names. If there's a lot of vandalism or drunken driving, it gets an editorial. But I'm worried about the impersonality of justice and of the police. We've got to stay *human!*"

As justice of the peace, he tries. That's one of his extra jobs. Others he holds or has held since coming to Bashaw in 1957 include Scout leader, Chamber of Commerce president, fire chief, Red Cross worker, undertaker's assistant, the clown in the July 1st parade, member of numerous planning committees, and preacher.

"Volunteer work is a part of life here," he told me. "Our minister said: 'Ron, I need some cobalt treatment—you take over.' So I preached for six weeks.

"You live," Ron explained, "and if you live, you owe other people for living."

He sees his newspaper, not as a "throw-away, but as proof to the community that it exists."

Over the years, Newsom has also done a good deal of fighting. Among the major results are a new 30-bed hospital, a new old-age home, a rejuvenated fire brigade, a much more active Chamber of Commerce, and Junior Citizen awards for three local youngsters. At the time I was there, he was concerned with getting a nursing-home and total-health-care survey done of the area.

His advice on fighting for something is: "Be well-prepared and don't be scared. If you have the truth—especially about the government—stand by it. Once you're sure, drive, push, involve people, and keep going."

The brown eyes rolled up to the paint peeling on the ceiling. "I have principles," he said. "If I can't live by them, I don't want to live. I'm an ethical bastard."

Much of the battling is done in editorials, of course. Newsom writes an average of eight per issue.

"I try to gear most of them to the community's conscience," he said. "I can justify every phrase I write...though not always every word."

He dug up some samples. Many were on serious topics and urged people to think and act and take care of each other. Some were tinged with sadness and showed a terrible longing for the world to be good, for pain and pettiness to be gone.

But there are some like these:

In June, 1968: "It's about time we men went down the street like the women, and displayed our clothes that give us a bold out-feeling.

"We're all for red socks, red ties, fluorescent clothes of any kind. It makes us feel good—and to the ladies that indicates either a guy who is hep, or a nut. We couldn't care less what they think. We like it."

And a year later: "We see men's ties have taken a turn again back to a width that at least can have some design. We do wish they'd bring back some diamond socks."

So he liked colour. "Can't get enough of it," said Ron. "Even my nightshirts are red with white stripes and yellow."

"Nightshirts?!"

"Yes. Myrtle sews 'em for me."

Newsom has won a number of awards for his editorials and other aspects of the paper. "They come as flowers," he said. The family has been reporting and printing in Alberta for a long time. His grandfather ran the *Lacombe Globe* for a while and later the *Claresholm Review*; his father worked on papers in Stavely, Didsbury, Banff, and Red Deer, where his son was born.

Ron's course was probably set at 13 with this sentence: "Crack! sounded the pistol and they were off...." He had to start an essay with it, and the teacher said it was the best she'd read in four years. Soon after high school, he got a job hand-setting in Claresholm at $1.25 a week. He worked on eight papers, one of which he owned, before settling in Bashaw. During the Second World War, he saw a lot of action in Europe. Towards the end, he edited part of the Canadian army paper, *The Maple Leaf*, in Brussels.

Up went the eyebrows: "I've worked hard, made no bucks, and had more fun than a 100-year-old."

He rose and zipped on a fire-red windbreaker with "Ron" lettered on the right sleeve.

"I'd like you to meet some townspeople," he said. "I don't give a damn what they say about me."

He needn't have worried.

We wandered down Bashaw Avenue. He showed me the shelf in Bob Whitecotton's haberdashery that holds a stuffed replica of every bird in the district. We said hello to Dick Miller, the baker, who came from Denmark 28 years ago. We visited the fire station. The hats and coats of the 19-man volunteer brigade were neatly ranged along the wall behind the trucks; Ron's number was 12. Nursing director Doreen Aasen gave us a quick tour of the hospital, where the editor stopped to examine a new incubator on behalf of which he had editorialized.

We dropped in on the home for the aged. We drove out to the farm of Henry Rutz, the mayor of Bashaw. Back in town we looked in on Earl Berry, owner of the Commercial Hotel and president of the Chamber of Commerce. He offered to show us Bashaw from the air in his Cessna 182. Ten minutes later, we were over the town's elevators, heading south to Buffalo Lake.

I asked each person we visited about Newsom. They seemed to think the question was an odd one, maybe because the answer was a foregone conclusion. "A hell of a good guy," was the gist of their replies.

Myrtle had a late lunch waiting—macaroni casserole. A pretty, round-faced woman, she and Ron have three children, two working, and one in college. She had a way of giving knowing winks while telling an anecdote, or when Ron did, which made a visitor feel at home. Myrtle recalled how Ron had nearly cried when he got his special weekly-editor's award. She mentioned that every Monday and Tuesday an elderly retired man comes to fold the papers at the shop. "He doesn't want any money," she said, "and he won't let anyone else do the job." And she told of a lady who kept a scrapbook of all the weddings in town over the last 25 years.

Ron asked if I wanted to come along to a threshing party at Frank Weines's place that afternoon. Weines farmed 360 acres, mostly wheat, and also ran the bar in the hotel.

The party was going strong when we got there. Entire families had come to help; the beer was served in pitchers.

On the way back I gathered these last bits of data from the *Star*'s editor: When he died he didn't want anything but "a light-coloured casket and some roses for the family"; he was working on a book, "My Town," a composite of all the Alberta communities he had lived in; he had no desire whatsoever to be the editor of a big-city paper; and he loved poetry, painting, music, gardening, and brown-bread and Spanish-onion sandwiches.

On the life of a small-town newspaper editor, Newsom said this: "You'll never make a lot of money. But I think only social work can give you as much satisfaction. Your judgment will expand, your capacity for compassion will grow."

But he put it better, I thought, when Bashaw's elevators showed up in our headlights. "You get to know your country like a book," he said. "Every road is a chapter. You know where everybody lives and you know why. When you come home you see the elevators. There they stand. There's been no fire. Nothing major has happened. It's OK."

That night in room 6 in the Commercial Hotel I was standing under the shower when there was a knock on the door. "Who's there?" I yelled.

"The *Bashaw Star*, sir!" called a high voice.

I splashed to the door and opened it a crack. An ink-stained hand came through holding a brown paper bag.

"This is for your own personal pleasure," said Ron Newsom.

It was a bottle of rye.

Chapter 15

"Not in Our Lifetime, or Our Children's Lifetime, Will We See the End of This Pollution"

It's such a big land this, and so much of it is unused, you would think that if a little of it got wrecked, a sliver really, it wouldn't matter that much....

The newspaper stories and television reports somehow never conveyed what it's actually like. Maybe they just *couldn't*, as *these* words may not either. The first time you see it, and the second and third and fourth times, all you can do is mutter, "My God. My God."

The only way to find out, really, is to travel down to Chedabucto Bay on Cape Breton, 190 miles northeast of Halifax. That's where the Liberian tanker, *Arrow*, hit Cerebrus Rock on 4 February 1970, broke in two, and spilled about half of the nearly four million gallons of her cargo. It was Bunker C oil, the thickest dregs of the oil-refining process.

Go to Isle Madame on the east side of the bay—locals call it Oil Madame, and its western shore is one of the worst hit areas—and take a walk along the rocky shore by any of the tiny old fishing communities like Arichat, West Arichat, Janvrin Harbour, or Petit de Grat. Wear rubber boots because your walk is through the filthiest black goo imaginable. It covers, in globs or as if painted, boulders, gravel, sand, and rock cliffs where waves have plastered it as high as 30 feet. If there's a patch that looks clean, try turning a few stones and see what's beneath. It has seeped deep down. Take a stick and poke the matted clutches of eelgrass the tide has brought in. With your finger, touch it oozing down the hull of a beached boat. There's a word for the shore you're walking on. The word is obscene.

The sliver of land takes up about one half of Chedabucto Bay's 150 miles of coastline, and it matters very much to fisherman Alfred Boudreau of West Arichat. There are a couple of thousand like Alfred around the bay. Most of them make between $3,500 and $4,500 a year. One way or another, they have all been, or will be, affected by the oil. That really goes for all the people in the area. And these people haven't been heard of much.

Alfred's main complaint is that he used to set 75 traps around where the wreck occurred, and can't set any there now. "For two nights I set 20 traps there as a test for the department of fisheries," he says. "I got lots of oil on my ropes and buoys but not one lobster. They promised full compensation, but that wasn't enough proof for it, I guess. They want me to dump in all 75 traps and get 'em oiled up."

He figures he'll lose between $500 and $600.

What's happened matters a whole lot to Alfred's neighbour, Henry Dorey, who hasn't had a steady job in two years. He does "a couple of days' work here, a couple there." He watches his eight kids line up for a *Weekend* photograph. He knows that it matters to Julia, Clarence, Edna, Tom, Nancy, Ivan, and even the two-year-old twins, Collette and Colleen. There'll be no swimming in the bay this summer, and he doesn't have a car to take them to a clean beach.

Isle Madame is a quiet, pretty place. About 15 miles long and seven wide, it has a population of 5,000. Life is slow and people haven't learned to be suspicious yet. They refer to the land across the bay as Nova Scotia. It's off the main tourist route, which runs along the Trans-Canada Highway toward the Cabot Trail. Most of the people are Acadians, descendants of the French uprooted by the fall of Louisbourg in 1758, and Huguenots from the Channel Isle of Jersey. French is still the first language of Isle Madame. There are no violent colours, except in autumn when the hardwoods turn brilliant red and orange and yellow. But the shingled homes are white, soft yellow, pale green, or unpainted and weathered. Artists visit here a lot. Except for the Saturday night Legion dance and the occasional movie, people come here in summer for the clam digging, swimming, and shore-walking. So Doug and Viola Shaw, who run the Isle Madame Motel in Arichat, also think the dirty water and beaches matter. Viola thinks it won't hurt business this year because the tourists will come to look at the oil. But what about next year?

And it matters to Ernest and Leonard Marchand, who run the only other motel in Arichat, *and* Isle Madame, the Marbro. A lot of the men working to clean up the oil stay here and there are black clots on the rugs in the rooms and black smears on the shower curtains. But the brothers will be compensated for that and anyway since "it" happened, what with the oil workers and visiting press, they've had 90 percent occupancy. But, again, what'll happen next year?

Father Alexander Poirier also is concerned. A native of the island, he's been the priest in Arichat for 25 years. He doesn't have a housekeeper so he eats out a lot. For the sake of diplomacy he eats one month in the one motel, the next month in the other. Father Poirier makes these comments:

"The scientists who have come here to work on the oil have great respect for the fisherman's knowledge. He may not have the technical education but he knows that water out there. That's *his* water.

"The people here enjoy themselves in abundance and in poverty—they've had both. If this had happened 25 years ago it would have been a different story. More people lived off fishing then."

The oil matters to Jean Dugas, an 89-year-old widow who lives in West Arichat. Her husband, a cook on a tugboat, fell overboard and drowned 57 years ago. She bakes her own bread and does all the housework for the two sons who live with her. "It's terrible, that stuff," she says. "It keeps getting all over the cat and I have to wash her with gasoline."

A few miles south, on the windy wharf in Little Anse, fishermen Francis and Clarence Samson, cousins and 62 and 63 respectively, are unloading the day's catch of 1,400 pounds of cod. They've been up since 3 AM, and are really too busy to stand around talking. No, the oil hasn't cost them any money yet. "Not *yet*," says Clarence.

In a cove near Arichat, fisherman Raymond Goyetche, a bachelor, has beached his boat and is trying to get the oil off her with the help of young Napoleon de Coste. "First gotta scrape the heavy stuff," he says without looking up. "Then I'll wash her with kerosene. It'll take a week."

In that week, presumably, Raymond won't be fishing.

Michael Greenham from Dartmouth runs the "slick-licker" *Gillian K* near White Side to the north of the island. The slick-lickers, brought in by the federal clean-up force, are scows fitted with terry-cloth-on-canvas conveyor belts at the bow. A part of the task force, he's been on the job for several months now, without a break, seven days a week, 18 to 20 hours a day. He works right along with his men digging into the mess with gloved hands and easing it along the licker. "I've seen a lot of oil," he says, "but never anything like this."

Tom Boudreau, who used to be a fisherman but is now a janitor at the school in Arichat, takes me out in his boat to look at the wreck. His friend Geoffrey de Coste, also a janitor, goes along for the ride. From a distance I can see the *Arrow*'s radar mast sticking out of the water. It's hard to imagine *why* she ever had to hit Cerebrus Rock. The bay must be big enough to hold the entire United States Navy without a single ship ever getting near the rock.

According to the *Arrow*'s captain, George Anastasopolous, who testified at an enquiry in May, his ship had a number of serious navigational defects at the time of the grounding. Among them, the radar set wasn't functioning properly; the echo sounder, used to determine water depth, wasn't working at all, and the gyro compass did not give the ship's true course.

Over on Janvrin Island, they've perhaps had more oil than anybody. Clancy George, 49, takes me to meet his father, Clinton, 79. "Dad'll die fishing," says Clancy.

Spry and lean, Clinton has been fishing for 65 years and is up every morning at 5. He has six children and 21 grandchildren. Today is Mother's Day and the entire family has gathered at Grandpa's and Grandma's. Clinton says that yesterday, together with a dozen herring, he caught a porpoise and a seal in the same net. They are covered with oil and maybe I'd like to see them down by the boat. "The oil is a terrible, terrible curse," he says on the way.

And when he shows me the black corpses, he says: "It's the end of the fishing here. I can't even get any herring for bait."

Others on the island say pessimistic things like that: "Not in our lifetime, or our children's lifetime, will we see the end of this pollution."

"There's not enough money in Canada to really clean this place up."

"We don't need nuclear wars, we'll just pollute ourselves to death."

Joe Kehoe of Rockie Bay, on the east side of Isle Madame where the oil hasn't penetrated, is 50 years old and has 11 children. He has 600 lobster traps out and claims he's going to lose about half of his lobster income, or $3,000.

And finally, the ruined sliver of land matters a lot to Adolph Kehoe from Petit de Grat. Adolph fished full time, until three years ago when he felt catches were declining. Now he sells life insurance. During the 17 days before the task force came in, the fishermen feared the government would just go bungling along and they'd be left in their misery. They organized themselves into the Association of Concern for the Chedabucto Bay area. They elected Adolph president.

He's a big, calm, thoughtful man. "At first everybody was really scared, but that wore off," he remembers. "They saw the task force pumping the oil out of the wreck, cleaning it off the waters, working on the beaches.

"It's much better now [early May] than a month ago. It was terrible, then. This thick, heavy, gooey stuff three or four feet deep on the beaches. I think 'shocking' would be a good word.

"Kids used to swim in Petit de Grat harbour, but not this summer. You can't walk on the beach. They're cleaning up the priority beaches where the tourists go, but where local kids swim sometimes aren't priority beaches. I've got two and we used to just send 'em down....It only takes a handful of the junk. They'll never be able to clean all the coastline affected. This could go on for years and years. Not even the experts know.

"It's like a disease. You learn to live with it."

As spokesman for the association, Adolph has done a lot of talking about the oil—and thinking about it: "The people of Canada, the people of the world, should take a hard look at what's happened here," he says. "What we risk destroying is the last frontier—the oceans. Eventually the food to feed the people of the earth is going to have to come from there. If we start ruining that source now, even before we've begun developing it, we're going to destroy mankind.

"They're now building 250,000-ton tankers. The *Arrow* was only 11,000 tons and we got only half her load. Think of what would happen if we got 50 times as much!

"Carrying these enormous loads of oil is the greatest deal in the world economically. But there's a moral side to it, too. We're risking the source of food for millions of people in the future. So, maybe we should say the hell with the oil. Carry it in pipelines or something—anyway, find some other solution.

"Maybe a lot of good will come out of the *Arrow*. Maybe it's an eye opener...."

Chapter 16

Of Pies and Chips and Pillow Slips and Cabbages and Things

It was, to tell the truth, a long week. It never rained and the sun easily beat the occasional chill wind. Like a touch of the whip, a bit of nastiness might actually have hurried these September [1972] days along, but it stayed fine. And right from the start, the hours slowed down until, by Sunday, time seemed barely to move at all. Sometimes this happens in a dream, and it isn't something you can fight.

On the first day I tried to keep time going at a decent clip—marched into Hants County Exhibition determined to get to its heart's matter fast, big-town man doping out a small town's doings. But the old man at the entrance spoiled it. He had to stamp the back of my hand with an illegible word in purple ink so that, if I wanted, I could leave the grounds for lunch, supper, too, and get back in again.

Stranger, hmmm? From where? Flew in, and drove up from Halifax? First time in Windsor? Nice town. Judge Haliburton wrote the Sam Slick stories here. And this Nova Scotia agricultural fair was the oldest in North America. Going, pretty well, since 1765. I didn't by the way, have to eat away, said the old man at the gate. They served a good meal here. Choice between fried chicken and ham, he thought. "Well, have a good time, friend," he said. "There's a lot to see."

He was the first to slow me up, to poke a hole through the old sail, so to speak. Eventually, I lowered it altogether and just drifted. It was, out there at Hants County Exhibition, the only way to go.

But I didn't learn that right away; nor, for that matter, did I realize that there was a lot to see. The fact is, I did the fair in the next two hours, including a stop for ice cream and one for a French fries with ketchup. Looked in on the buildings and stables, about an acre walled and roofed. Saw the 40-odd commercial exhibits, from televisions to tombstones. Checked beef and dairy cattle, oxen, draft horses, and sheep. Visited the exhibits of vegetables, field and fruit crops, honey, school and household crafts, flowers, and the best work of the area's 4-H members. Saw some horse showing and jumping, and an act with boxer dogs playing basketball with balloons in the roofed hockey rink. And finally, I toured the midway at back of the fair's 41 acres. All in two hours. There merely remained ox-pulling and tug-of-war in the evening.

The two men handling first-prize cucumbers, I think, were the ones who did it. Dressed in dark suits, white shirts, and hard-knotted, narrow ties, they stood for the longest time at that one spot. The cucumbers were fat, long, and shiny. The men fondled them, weighed them in square-fingered hands, and talked in low voices. Then they moved on, one step, to the cauliflowers. First to read the winning grower's name on the tag, then to touch and comment again. Slowly, slowly, they made their way around that vegetable exhibit, the size of a small field and smelling of earth, having a good time. You get thirsty when you see others drink, so I followed the two to see what was so great about onions, and green beans, beets, carrots, cabbages, broccoli, potatoes, lettuce, green peppers, turnips, tomatoes, and corn. I didn't find out the first time around. But on trips in the days that followed, I did: the stuff on that table was beautiful. I wished I had grown some of it. I wondered what it would be like, for instance, to be Danny Dill, aged five, and to have won first prize for the heaviest squash at Hants County Exhibition—165 pounds!

The cucumber men showed the pleasure there is in looking at another's pride. Obviously, most visitors, the majority of them farm folk, knew already; it was one big reason for coming. The other reason was explained to me by David Coombes, the fair's

31-year-old secretary-manager: "It's a time for people to get together. Nobody would ever miss it. When I was a boy on the farm I took the whole week off from school."

Why were there no signs in town directing you to the fair? David Coombes looked puzzled. "What for? Everybody knows where it is."

I noted—and maybe it's like that at all country fairs—a lot of elderly couples holding hands, a lot of young couples holding hands, and a lot of families holding hands. I didn't see many people alone. I heard one woman say to another: "Some people here look as if they own the whole world." This fitted especially a boy and girl in their late teens riding slowly across the grounds, bare back on a horse, each holding a bottle of beer. I observed that most people had dressed up for the occasion, like the cucumber men. And, like those two, they knew how to look and enjoy.

So I followed people, again and again, past African violets, sweet peas, gladiolas, roses, geraniums, asters, petunias, miniature gardens, plums, apples, pears. I followed people to the Ruff 'n' Ready gift shop where the secret of how to get a boat into a bottle was learned. I followed them past cakes, cookies, pie crusts, muffins, rolls, banana bread, rock collections, cushions, candles, sweaters, mitts, lamps, candy dishes, towels, pottery, dresses, birdhouses, tool boxes, floor mats, rocking chairs, cheese boards, nightgowns, handbags, toy animals, scrapbooks, tie racks, paintings, bedspreads of crocheted wool, embroidered pillow slips, a towel with the Lord's Prayer cross-stitched on it. Hand-sewn children's dresses, pictures in needlepoint, pickles, jams, scarves, quilted blankets, hooked rugs, fudge, and doughnuts. And more.

It was different in the big barn, where the chorus of oxen bells was like a Thailand symphony. No longer did I have to follow people around. Here there was expert guidance from the likes of Bob Johnston, 58, who drove the Clydesdale hitch for Wilson Equipment of Truro, Nova Scotia. Larger than life, somehow, was Bob, with a big head and a voice of thunder. Buried in his massive chest, ironically, was a little machine called a pacemaker to help his weakened heart. He used to be a blacksmith, he told me. He had shown his own horses every year since 1938 at the Hants Ex. Then came two heart attacks in quick succession and the smithy went to his son, and the horses were sold. Luckily, the Wilson people hired him to drive their three-pair hitch of Clydes at fairs around the East from June till November.

"It's a disease, these horses," Bob roared. "Some fellows go after women, or drink, or boats, or hunting. With me, it's horses!"

Once, just before taking his team in front of the people—only a two-pair hitch, a mere 10,000 pounds of horse and harness—I saw him take a small nip of brandy. "MEDICINE!" he bellowed. High up on the yellow wagon, behind the four immense rear ends, his flask tilted to his mouth, ho looked like something straight out of a marvelous folk tale.

From Bob to farmer Leon Taylor, 38, and also a Clydesdale man. Red-haired and stocky, Leon said that, besides his two Clydes at the fair, there were five more at home. At most, he admitted, you could hope to break even with prize money, but usually you lost. It was all for the fun of it. "It gets in your blood." His father, William, had been showing at the fair for 50 years. He was one of the white-haired, weathered men always around in the barn, smoking and talking cattle or horses. Come night, some shared beer or rum with younger fellows and sang sad Maritime songs.

"Warm," I heard one of these men greet an even older friend one afternoon.

"No, not warm...." the second corrected him. Then, after a pause, "Muggy!"

Leon said that the week at the fair was even harder work than at home. Washing, grooming, harnessing, and showing the animals could go from 4 AM till midnight. "After driving a four-hitch, my arms'll ache for an hour. It's like hanging onto a 100-pound bag of feed."

Leon's brother Paul, 17, could usually be found with Duke and Darb, his young oxen of 1,480 pounds weight combined. He'd shown before when still in his 4-H club, but these were the first he had ever owned. He let no one else look after them. This year, expertly waving his whip over their heads, he walked, turned, and stopped the beasts to win a second prize.

"I come here for a good time," he told me. "I don't come to win.

"When you come into an exhibition, you give on you don't know nothing. Then guys who know tell you all sorts of things. You pick up a lot of stuff."

Sure enough, minutes later, an old-timer tipped him off on how to fix the oxen's brass horn tips more securely with sandpaper.

At night the hockey rink filled up for the tugs of war, oxen pulls, horse jumping, singers, and musicians. Alana Payne, who is Miss Windsor and also Miss Nova Scotia, sang for a while. Thanking her, Mayor Eric Nott said three times in his brief speech, "Alana, we're 100 percent behind you!"

The contests of brute strength of both men and oxen seemed dull at first. A dozen or more yokes of oxen, would, each in turn, drag thousands of pounds of weight 18 inches at a time. More weight was added until only the strongest pair could move it.

And so with the two 10-man, tug-of-war teams, each pulling a thick rope in opposite directions for as long as 15 minutes. There seemed a terrible sameness about these events. That is, until you learned of the many strict rules for both, and until a tall thin man wearing suspenders said: "This is part of our heritage. It's a good thing these men keep it up." After that, you strained along with the men and the animals.

Some of the spectators were there for the first time that week, but many of the people I talked to, watched *every* night, and perhaps later went back to the barn or somebody's trailer for a sip and talk.

So, by the end of Sunday, a weary Paul Taylor, shovelling behind Duke and Darb, said it perhaps for all: "I'm tired. We're all tired—the horses, too. I'm not sorry it's over."

It was easy for him to say, because he'll be back next year.

Chapter 17

The Only Human Tracks
for Miles Around

"A trapper," said Magnus Nyman, "keeps his skinning knives sharp." He picked one from a dozen hanging along a wall log in his cabin and sharpened it on a strip of aluminum-oxide paper. To test the edge, he shaved some hairs from his wrist. Then he set to cleaning the inside of a freshly skinned beaver pelt—the fat came off like warm butter. Something else learned about trapping.

Magnus had supplied a lot of information like that. And he had told me about his environment, background, beliefs, etc. It had all been interesting, truthful—he has smoked seven cigarettes in his life and probably told as many lies—and useful. But there was one thing I had yet to learn from him. We had tramped for hours through the woods, shared meals, talked late several nights, but I still didn't understand *why* Magnus chose to live as he did. There aren't many like him left in Canada—and tomorrow I would leave.

Magnus worked quickly and surely. Though a familiar chore, it still took some concentration and muscle. At 67, you would think he might breathe a little faster, but no. The stove hissed and snapped and the air above it trembled, but there was not the faintest shine of sweat on the man's head. Now he scraped away at the hide and whistled through his teeth.

For a while he didn't speak. Whenever he did, he would stop scraping. With him, it was one thing or the other, scrape or talk. Anyway, he rarely began a conversation. He isn't used to it. Most of the time he lives alone. Human voices, even his own, aren't a common sound. A few years back, he would talk to his dog. But the dog got old and Magnus shot it, and he never talks to himself.

Evening was coming—his favourite time of day. In summer, the short, stocky man makes sure he's out in a canoe then, just drifting and watching. But it was March [1973]. So he put on a thick red hunting shirt, took a rifle scope, and wandered out onto the lake below his cabin and, turning slowly, scanned the land. He would stay out for 20 minutes. The setting sun gave substance to his tracks. They were the only tracks....

All human tracks, for miles and miles around, are those of Magnus. His kingdom—he and he alone can run the registered trap lines on the Crown land—measures 100 square miles. It's silent, frozen wilderness, about 200 miles north of Sault Ste Marie, Ontario. The nearest town is Chapleau, 45 miles east. If Magnus were to break a leg, that might be tough. Or merely inconvenient; he would manage all right. He's worked those trap lines since 1962. Before that, he trapped further north at Fire River for 30 years. He lives all year round in the woods: trapping in winter, guiding fishermen and hunters in summer and fall.

To get to his "headquarters"—he's built four other cabins around the territory—you can walk in four miles from a highway, which also means crossing several lakes, or fly in from Chapleau.

I did the latter. Only just before landing, could I spot the tiny pine-log structure on the spit of land sticking into the ice. It was a bright and windless day. The Cessna 185 immediately took off again. The moment its roar had died the awesome silence started to sing in my ears. Nothing moved. Every sound was my own, and it was *noise*.

There's a sign on a corner of Magnus' house that says "Beware of Bear Traps." There are no traps, but he put it there because a few years ago some people stole all the gas he had.

There's a main room with the stove in it, a small room for drying skins, and one for sleeping. Windows are sealed with transparent plastic sheets. All the furniture is homemade. On the walls, hang tools, traps, rifles, snowshoes, rolls of wire, and a dog harness.

Shelves in a corner hold canned and dehydrated foods. From the ceiling dangle poles on wires with socks and trousers drying from them. Oddly, the most handsome thing in the house is a peacock mounted by Magnus himself. A weasel got in once and tried to eat its throat. The silliest thing is an electric clock set forever at noon.

Magnus, with his slightly stern mouth and blue eyes, let it be known that he didn't like spending much time inside during the day. The end of the season was near, and he still had a number of traps out. The snow was hard, so no need for snowshoes. That's how he gets around most of the winter, though, or on skis; much of the terrain is too rugged for the snowmobile. In summer, of course, he travels by canoe. He has five stashed here and there.

We trudged along for about two miles, crossing several lakes, a marsh, and a stream. The land looked lifeless until Magnus started pointing things out: fresh lynx droppings, skunk tracks, a partridge, a squirrel, a raven. He cited the name of every tree and bush and type of rock, of every fish under the ice, of every winged thing expected in the spring. He moved at incredible speed and often had to stop to wait for me. The stream of information was shouted over his shoulder. Axe in hand, packsack and rifle on his back, he walked with a roll, hunched forward, head swinging from side to side, missing nothing.

"I'm a lot safer here than on city streets! There's nothing in the forest to fear—only to respect!

"I can't sleep in the city. Here I can fall asleep anywhere."

Born and raised in Finland, and schooled in Swedish, he came to Canada in 1927, but has retained the Scandinavian's drawn-out vowels and never conquered the tricky "th."

"How many lakes do you have?" I called.

"One hundred!"

Then I stopped him and asked for an up-to-date count of some of the animal life on his land.

"Eight bears, 12 moose, three timber wolves, 38 beaver colonies, 12 to 13 otters, 50 marten, two fishers, three lynx, 75 mink, about 1,000 rabbits, 100 muskrat, 35 to 40 foxes, 70 weasels. By fall, all figures will have about doubled."

When we got to one of his traps, Magnus showed how he had placed it at a spot in the beaver dam in need of repair. A worker was bound to show up, did, and the trap had snapped shut over his neck killing it instantly.

Magnus mostly uses the Conibear trap, the most humane and effective one developed thus far. (According to Lloyd Cook, president of the Canadian Trappers' Federation, most trappers use it today and only use the leg-hold traps where the animal will be quickly drowned—in about two minutes.)

Magnus said he would show me an old Indian trick. He sharpened the end of a two-inch twig and pushed it through one nostril of the dead beaver and out the other. Around the twig he looped the end of a rope. He flopped the beaver on its back and it dragged neatly behind him.

"We have to be more conscious of trapping in a humane way," he said. "In the early years I wasn't so conscious....I don't want to see that animal suffer. If I can't kill it quickly, I won't kill it.

"We only take the surplus crop of animals. I harvest them where there are too many and there's a shortage of food. If I didn't there would be sickness and starvation.

"I believe one car running one mile does more harm than I do in one year in the woods. God put those animals there for us to use. As long as women think they look nice in fur, I'll be in business. And that'll be a long time yet...I hope."

We made several similar trips during my stay, but Magnus trapped only one more beaver. As we got to the dam where he had set his trap, he suddenly started running. He leapt onto the dam's narrow top, risking a fall into open water. In the centre he leaned forward, axe over his head, very still, then slammed it down.

His face was dark red. I remember him saying that he couldn't recall ever having been really angry in his life. "It was alive!" he cried. "*Alive!*"

He yanked the trap and beaver out of the water. The steel had shut over the animal's middle not its neck. Magnus said it must have swum in a minute before. It would certainly have drowned in a few more. Still, the trap had not worked properly. On the way back he hardly said a word.

I asked Magnus once if he had any major regrets. As usual, he stopped whatever he was doing, and picked his words. Yes, at 16 he had had the chance to get more schooling and had passed it up.

He was sorry about that. And: "When he was a pup, my last dog kept jumping on my snowshoes and then I would dive into the snow. It went on all day and I was tired. So I took a stick and spanked him. I'll never forgive myself for that. I promised myself I would never give an animal pain again."

———•◦•◦•———

It was dark when Magnus came back up from the lake on that last night. He was whistling "Red River Valley"; usually, he whistled tunelessly. He pumped the gas lantern, lit it, and finished cleaning the pelt. Then he cooked supper—canned spaghetti and coffee. Much of his food, in winter at least, is canned. We ate without saying much. That afternoon we had made our longest hike and done a lot of talking—without a hint of the "why" I was after.

We had crossed five lakes to reach the one holding the traps. All were empty. Magnus had shown me the one that had clamped shut over a chewed stick a beaver had obviously been swimming with in his mouth. The beaver escaped.

Magnus had built a small fire at the lake's edge beside a beaver portage. He had brought the makings for tea. As on the first day, there was no wind, it was warm, and the lake's surface glittered.

"The wolf," Magnus had observed, "is the most difficult to trap. He's cunning and almost never curious. The fox is very curious. The most intelligent animal is not the dog, nor the horse. It's the otter."

He'd stared across the lake. "The sky is blue and all the trees are beautiful."

The lake was about the size of a city block. Did it have a name? No, it had no name. How about Hillen Lake? Yes, fine, that could be its name. But Magnus suspected there were no more beavers here and if that were true, it was unlikely another human being would come by in the next 15 to 20 years.

"It would be nice to know," he'd said, "the names of all the little wild flowers that come up in spring. I've never had time for that."

To ship furs and fetch supplies and mail, Magnus goes into Chapleau about every two weeks. Occasionally he takes a holiday. Two years ago he went home to Finland. But most of the time he is alone. Twenty of the 40 Christmases spent in the bush, were celebrated alone.

"But people in the city are just as lonesome," he had said. "Here, at least, I like everything I see.

"The first time I wanted to get married was in the 30s. I didn't think I could support a wife the way I wanted to. The second time, well, you get older, more selfish....There were disagreements. I guess I have never been truly in love...so in love I would have done anything. Yes, sometimes the lonesomeness bothers me a little."

After supper, Magnus immediately rinsed the dishes. He also shaves every day, hardly ever takes a drink, doesn't curse, rises at 6 and goes to bed around 8, fills a tub once a week for a bath, keeps his nails neatly trimmed, and, when he attends a trappers' convention, he leaves before the dancing. He likes telling stories though.

There was the 110-pound drunken doctor from Sudbury whom he had guided on a three-day fishing trip. The doctor brought whisky and rum and two Spanish onions, which he wasn't allowed to eat at home.

At one point they had to portage. Magnus, already carrying all the equipment and food, had to take care of the 82-pound aluminum canoe as well. The doctor followed empty-handed, singing. Then a muffled shout:

"Magnus!"

Magnus turned and there lay the doctor face down in a pile of moose droppings.

"What are these, Magnus?" asked the doctor looking up.

"You know what they are."

"I don't."

"Moose droppings."

"Magnus, you could sell these as fertilizer and tell people they'll grow the biggest flowers. Magnus, you'll make a fortune!"

Well, maybe the doctor had something....That doctor never fished once. He drank and watched Magnus fishing.

"Magnus," said the doctor, "if you can make me forget sick people while I'm here—I'm happy."

And the one about the two bull moose that chased Magnus into a lake....And speaking of moose, Magnus right then went out under the stars and through a birch-bark horn did his imitation of a lovesick cow moose which many a bull has regretted. The echo of the sad and painful grunts came back from across the lake.

Thus we spent the last evening.

Magnus mentioned that he had once received a letter from the private secretary of King George VI. The King and Queen visited Canada just before the Second World War broke out in 1939. Magnus took some pictures of the royal couple and later mailed copies to the King. Hence the letter, which he looked for but couldn't find. But this is what it says in a book called *Merry America*, a day-by-day account of the tour.

Monday, June 5th
The whole of Fire River's population, namely 12 persons, turned out to welcome the King and Queen when the royal train drew up for servicing. Amongst them was a trapper, Mr Magnus Nyman, to whom the Queen spoke immediately after their Majesties descended.

"How cold is it in Fire River during the winter?" she asked.

"Sixty-five below," he replied, "and the snow, she's six feet deep!"

"Good heavens," said the King.

Towards the end of the evening, Magnus, finally, gave an explanation, if not a very complete one, of why he lives his particular way.

"Trappers won't survive," he said. "Fewer and fewer are willing to live this life. So many I used to know in the old days have dropped out. They're still living, but in town where they can have it softer. I'm very independent. I've never asked for relief or help from anybody. I've never stuck out my hand.

"I'm sure I'll live in the woods until I'm 100, and probably a lot longer."

But maybe he had actually said it all when I first entered his home and noticed a battery-powered radio on the table.

"Listen to it much?"

"No," Magnus said. "The news is always bad, isn't it? My news is written in the snow. It's printed there. It's always good news."

A Trapper's Balance Sheet

Of the 60,000 licensed trappers in Canada [in 1973], 35 percent work at it full-time, supplementing their income a little with guiding and fishing in the off-season. Magnus Nyman is one of these. Last year he sold 130 pelts and made around $6,000. His operating expenses, he said, came to about $1,000. An average trapper's investment he calculated at about $9,000—in his case, it includes five canoes, three outboard motors, one snowmobile, three power saws, and a supply of traps. There are, of course, no worries about electricity, water, or rent payments.

Seventy Million Canadians
Can't All Be Wrong

"Eaten any lobster yet?" she screeches as the stout woman plumps down beside her and the bus starts up again. It's her hello to a stranger. Sitting right behind me, she has screeched things all the way down from Campbellton, New Brunswick, where she got on at 2:30 PM. It's past 8 now and growing dark without let-up in the heat of this late-summer Sunday [1970]. Moncton, the end of the run, is another 20 miles south.

"Yes, for supper," says the stout woman comfortably. "I was visiting my cousin."

"Are they high?" the other woman shrills.

"Well, I expect they are. I didn't ask the price...."

"Lobster is high!"

"Well...."

"I have a daughter," she screeches. "She is married to an Englishman. *He can't stand lobster!*"

"Well," says the stout woman, "I'm sure they have other nice things in his country."

"Can't stand shrimp either!"

There's a silence as her neighbour thinks about this—as we *all* think about this.

She is in her late 60s, has a long nose, and tiny mouth, and her thick hair is pulled back into a bun. The first time I heard that voice, I shot around to look and got a hard, cold stare. She struck me as kind of witchy. But it was she who got them to fix the pop machine in Bathurst, the bathroom unlocked at a stop below

Newcastle, and it was she, along with Bill the driver, who helped blind Al to his seat. From her screeches we have learned she's a mother from Moncton; she's never been to Miami but has a calendar from there in her kitchen; she likes riding buses because the countryside is beautiful; and never mind her varicose veins, she's doing okay anyway. She comes on strong because of the voice, but she's maybe the nicest person on the bus. You can't tell about people. For instance last Thursday at the start of this trip....

Early morning, and the half-empty bus bounces along Quebec's old streets. In the seat ahead, two young nuns are giggling because they have to keep adjusting each other's headdresses. Across the aisle, two girls in bare feet with fringed leather pouches at their hips smoke without talking. Behind them, even though we've only just started, a bearded young guy in a wide floppy hat is curled up asleep.

The middle-aged gangster next to me lights a cigarette. I had noticed him in the Quebec terminal. He stood like a rock amid the noise and people hurrying with suitcases, babies, old mothers, and cartons tied with rope. A powerful, small man in a black suit and black hat shoved over an eye. Near him in the crowd swayed a tall, unshaven fellow in a zebra-stripe jacket. One leg of his trousers was ripped and a mickey stuck out of his back pocket. Every time the loudspeaker blared, his head jerked and he would lurch forward towards somebody to ask something, but people turned away. The blare sounded again. Zebra-stripe made a turn too fast and jackknifed over the gangster behind him. They talked and then the gangster led him outside to a bus that said Rivière du Loup. My bus.

Zebra-stripe is stretched out now on the long seat in back, snoring.

The gangster turns and smiles, showing six gold teeth. "Bonjour," he says.

"*Bonjour,*" I say, "*ah—Monsieur l'Abbé.*"

I guessed his age wrong too. He is 70. This is an important trip: He's going home to Rivière du Loup, 116 miles northeast of Quebec along the St Lawrence River, to celebrate the 50th year of his entering religious life. "My family will give a big party," he says. "Thirty people."

We've crossed the river and are roaring along its southern shore into one of the most scenic parts of Canada—the Gaspé Peninsula. Separating the lower St Lawrence River from the Gulf of St Lawrence, it's a huge thumb of mountains, valleys, rivers, and beaches. This is the oldest part of Canada: Jacques Cartier first stepped ashore here.

I'm going to bus 844 miles through 151 towns around the Gaspé and into New Brunswick as far as Moncton. This isn't a tour bus, but an ordinary inner-city one, the kind that stops anywhere you wave it down. Some 70 million people travelled on them in this country last year. It's relatively cheap, safe, and comfortable, and gets you almost anywhere in Canada. You have no traffic worries, you see much more than in a car, and you cut through communities trains never touch.

Now, and until we enter New Brunswick Sunday afternoon, we run almost continually along water—the St Lawrence, and later the gulf. Hillsides and groves of maples, white birch and fir, cliffs, beaches strewn with driftwood, cod nets spread to dry, old wooden houses, roadside shrines, children selling hand-carved sailing vessels, fishing villages, electric crosses on hilltops. The road climbs, swoops down to the shore, climbs again, and a new view leaps into focus. This goes on and on...but it isn't scenery you take home in your mind....

He is waiting for us outside St Roch des Aulnaies, where five more nuns get on. About four feet tall, maybe seven years old, he stands very still, unsmiling. Then he slowly raises his right hand to eye level, thumb up, index finger pointing. The finger is aimed at us and—pow! I count 14 like him in four days.

There's also a woman with red hair who climbs on at La Pocatière where the barefoot girls get off. Her body, in tight, purple silk, sighs as she sits down in the girls' seat. She's a big, good-looking woman, her piled red hair frozen with hair spray. This is what the priest and I learn:

A month ago she came back from a four-month visit to her daughter in Oakland, California, who is married to a black microbe researcher from Chicago. She got sick there and had to go to hospital, and, of course, she can't really speak English and, well, nobody in that hospital had ever seen a French woman before and they all came to look at her, the doctors, the nurses....What she didn't like, especially in Seattle, was the way all the girls dressed like go-go dancers, with a bit here, here, down here—disgusting. She has worked in this bar in Rimouski for 12 years but never in all that time has she taken one drink. Doesn't like it, and never did. But she has to admit it's pretty silly—12 years in a bar and never a drink. And she throws back all that red hair and laughs and the silk ripples and I don't believe her.

There are no rooms, says the Rivière du Loup taxi driver, except maybe in this one very old hotel. On the veranda, men in suspenders and straw hats sit in rocking chairs watching the street. Inside it's very still. Yellowed photographs of King George VI and Queen Elizabeth hang in the hallway. A hand-carved harmonium and four spittoons grace the lounge.

I'm told that in the evening one *must* visit the dance hall in the motel by the river. It's a dark, cavernous place, and packed. The four-man group belts out "Daughter of Darkness"; the singer's fluorescent shirt bobs about the stage. The bar holds 30 men, and, at the tables nearby, land the girls who've come on their own, cool and marvelously bored. Bernadette, in mini and see-through blouse, is behind the bar. There's a lot of slinging and running to do—but a smile comes with every beer. Bernadette smiles at strangers! More than that, she *touches* them. After 90 minutes, I note that she has served drinks, smiled, and briefly touched the hands or faces of at least 30 men. Not one pass has been made. There have been a dozen offers of drinks, but she says, No thank you she doesn't drink—and laughs and presses a hand. It's the red-haired woman from Rimouski all over again, but small and blonde and 30 years younger.

Anybody in the world can wave down a bus and, en route for Ste Anne des Monts this Friday morning, they do; often in the middle of nowhere. Three elderly ladies in slacks wave the bus down, a girl with a guitar does, a man with a pipe who is asked to put it out, two guys with beards and sleeping bags, a very bald man in a grey suit, a chic young woman with a baby, two little boys who look like each other, two girls with long hair, a Chinese man, a man and a boy holding hands—they all wave the bus down.

Just before Bic, which is just before Rimouski, the man holding the boy's hand leans over and says: "Bic is very beautiful, you know." He and the boy get out in Bic.

Médard, a 17-year veteran driver, takes over for the Rimouski-Ste Anne des Monts run. A big brown dog chases us in Matane. Médard recalls that he once had to lift a six-foot-one, 250-pound, paralyzed woman out of his bus all by himself. If he had lots of time, would he take a bus to, say, Vancouver? "I'd be crazy!" he yells. "I'm in a bus all the time!"

In Ste Anne des Monts, there is no "must" this evening, so I sit in a rocking chair on the hotel's veranda and watch the street. Towards 11 PM, the owner comes out. He says that a traveller alone is usually lonesome and if everybody kept that in mind there would be fewer lonesome travellers in this country—so how about a beer? We sit quietly and drink the beer.

"You must eat wild strawberry jam," he says suddenly. "Tomorrow. With breakfast." And he gets up and starts turning off lights.

It was superb, the jam, even at 6 AM.

Albert is at the wheel for the lap to Percé. Alone on the road near Ruisseau Castor, a boy with a little empty wagon stops and watches us gravely—it's another world going by.

The librarian from Ottawa taps me awake and says that I just missed a tractor burning in a field with a bunch of people standing around it doing nothing. She's on a tour of the Gaspé with her young niece. She speaks six languages and has travelled the world. In Gaspé there's a 15-minute stop. We buy ice cream cones and she says that when you pause briefly like this in a strange place, it's like coming home to get back in your bus again.

The few miles before entering Percé are the most spectacular of the trip—wild and mountainous. Percé is crammed with long-haired and short-haired tourists. The long hairs are suspicious of the short hairs and town folk and vice versa, and the mood is a bit sour.

Next morning we're almost empty as Albert starts her up for Campbellton: on board are two pale girls from Toronto and Linda, a mathematics teacher from Winnipeg. The Toronto girls haven't much to say; Linda sleeps. After a few towns, a woman with a crying baby gets on. A man sitting on the veranda of his house with a raven on his wrist, waves her goodbye. An old lady in a yellow hat waits at the Carlton Centre stop. Albert brakes, opens the door, but she just looks at us, not moving. When the bus starts up again, she waves her arms and starts running.

"You know," she tells him breathing hard, "I've been waiting two hours and now I almost missed you. Isn't that something?"

We switch buses in Campbellton, and the woman with the long nose gets in and sits down behind me. The driver's name is Bill and, as we pass his sister's house just outside town, he honks his horn. He honks at houses of friends and relatives all along the way. In Dalhousie, a cheerful small woman climbs aboard.

"So you're finally going home, eh?" says Bill.

"You stop teasing me," she says. "Just stop it. And you better hurry 'cause there's a funeral coming around by the English church and you're going to get stuck."

A bit later, a girl in a brown jumpsuit blowing bubble gum gets on, and blind Al. He's a huge man, white on top, and carries a big suitcase. Al sells things door to door around New Brunswick— shoelaces, combs, mirrors.

"Wait—I'll help you!" she screeches behind me. This is the first time I hear that voice, and I turn and get that cold, hard stare. Then she's up and guiding Al to a seat.

"When did you come up, Al?" Bill yells, moving again.

"Thursday," says Al.

"Yesterday?" yells Bill.

"Thursday!" yells Al. "Where were you Thursday, Bill?"

"Went the other way Thursday!" yells Bill.

"I'm sitting up front and Bill tells me he drives this road five days a week. "I know every hole—and usually hit them," he says and laughs.

There's a long screech from behind. She's laughing, too.

Bill passes a couple of shirtless kids on bicycles. He is whistling and then he shouts, "They say we're a hundred years behind every-body else down here!" and goes on whistling.

Now she lets us know that she's never been to Miami, but has a scenery calendar from there in her kitchen. Bill says his idea of nice scenery is a shapely blonde in a bikini.

At Richibucto, Bill announces a two-minute stop. "There's cold pop and a bathroom, folks."

A few miles outside Buctouche we're waved down by a clutch of teenage girls who, Bill says, are going to a dance there. "I wish I was young again to go dancing," he says.

"You come *on!*" she screams. "You're not too old!"

"That's what they *all* say!" yells Bill and he laughs a great laugh.

Just outside Moncton, an elderly, dignified man gets on. He sits down with me. "Well," he says softly, smiling, "she's warm, isn't she?"

"She's *hot!*" she screeches from behind.

We pile out in Moncton, sticky and tired, say thanks to Bill, and go our ways. She goes straight inside, makes for the nearest pay phone, deposits her dime, dials, and then that incredible, that fantastic voice fills the terminal:

"I'm here!"

Some Pointers on Bus Travel

• Get to the bus-stand early. Seating is on a first-come, first-serve basis.

• Try to avoid the rear. It gets the worst bumping.

• Try hard for a window seat.

• The preferred seat, because of the view, is the one to the right of the driver up front. But, it's also about the only seat where the passenger stays very aware of the traffic.

• Middle of the bus on the right is the best seating—least engine noise and traffic awareness.

• Talk to your neighbour—he or she probably won't come your way again.

• Go to the bathroom before you get on. Some buses don't have bathrooms and if they do it's a tricky business.

• If you're going on a long journey, try to plan it so you're never on the road for more than four hours or 200 miles a day—the ideal length for a bus trip.

• Don't bring reading material. The great advantage to travelling in a bus is sitting so high and getting to see so much of the country.

Chapter 19

Maintenance of Law and Order— and Double Parking

It wasn't deliberate nor probably typical, but I waited three-and-a-half days for Chief Ted Day of Exeter, Ontario, to do one really policeman-like thing.

We talked for hours in his tiny office, drank coffee in the restaurant next door, tooled around in the cruiser, and walked up and down Main Street. I watched him sell bicycle licences, drink rye and Coke in his yellow-brick home, greet dozens and dozens of people by name, win a few dollars one night at the races in London, 30 miles south, sit stiff and stern in magistrate's court, take reports from his three-man force, laboriously type his monthly report to council...and finally, yes, there was one small, concrete show of Maintaining Law and Order.

Day, of course, was perfectly capable. He's been a policeman for 19 years, 15 with London city force, which he left as a first-class detective, and nearly four as chief in Exeter [pop. 3,200 in summer 1972]. And he works hard at his job; the year before he arrived, 1968, the department investigated 436 occurrences and laid 17 Criminal Code charges; in 1969, it was 1,199 occurrences and 47 charges. Just the same, I felt that to get an idea of the life of a small-town cop I had to see Day in action.

Once or twice he came close. For instance, when the middle-aged woman in green trousers stormed into his station: "Damn!" she shouted, smacking the counter. "Why the ticket, chief? Since *when* can't I park at the IGA?"

"Since a week," said Day, who had immediately put on his cap.

"Blast it!" said the woman. "I've been driving 20 years. *Never* had a ticket!"

"Are you kidding me?" Day asked.

"Honest!" she said.

"Tell you what," Day growled. "Because it's the first time…but don't ever do it again—or I'll come *looking* for you!"

"Jeepers!" said the woman. "Thanks, Chief!"

But it hardly rated as a major law-and-order effort.

Ted Day is 46 years old, five feet 11 1/2 inches tall, and weighs 185 pounds. He has large feet, hands, and ears, curly iron-grey hair, and blue eyes. He has a lined, ruddy face, and a scar running across his nose, acquired in 1956, playing left wing on the London-police hockey team against the Detroit police. He has a deep, gravelly voice. He chuckles rather than laughs, lumbers rather than walks, and looks good in uniform. (The chuckle, incidentally, precedes his anecdotes. As a policeman he hears a lot of gossip. He is a discreet man, though, and often I just got the chuckle—no story. It was frustrating as hell.)

Whatever situation Day is in, he's usually in charge of it—and it shows. Authority fits like his starched blue shirt: he is the chief. Only at home, six miles north in Hensall, Bean Capital of the World, in the company of his vivacious, brown-eyed wife, Marion, four daughters and son, is Ted Day…just Ted Day.

The police station is in the town hall. Built in 1841, it also houses the fire department, council chambers, the works department, and a big room where old men play cards. Next year, Exeter's centennial, they're going to build a new town hall. Now, all that cheers Day's cubicle are a few group photographs of policemen. In one of them is his late father who started with the Regina force and later served eight years as chief in Meaford, Ontario, near Georgian Bay. In the crowded one-room main office, all that is of interest are a few mug shots on the wall. Off this room there are two narrow, one-night-only cells with wooden bunks and doors of steel.

When I arrived, Day told me the cells were waiting for a white man and an Indian from Winnipeg charged with trying to break into Exeter's Les Pines Hotel the previous weekend. The men were being held in jail in Walkerton 60 miles north. They would be fetched next morning for magistrate's court. If I liked, I could go along for the ride.

That first visit with Day lasted three hours and was only interrupted by a customer for a bicycle licence—

Chief: "Beautiful day, eh?"

Boy: "Uh-huh."

Chief: "Rain tomorrow though."

Boy: "Field day tomorrow."

Chief: "Tomorrow, eh?"

Boy: "Uh-huh."

Chief: "Well, thanks very much!"

And, once more, when Day put on his cap to go next door to get us a coffee. "If the phone rings," he instructed, "pick it up and say: 'Exeter police department. Would you hang on please?'" It didn't ring.

Exeter's four-man force, including the chief, measures just over 24 feet, weighs 816 pounds, and has 55 years of police experience. Besides Day, there are first-class constables Ardell "Mac" McIntyre, 43; John Cairns, 36; and George Robertson, 30. (I saw the constables do policeman-like things long before the chief did: McIntyre escorting prisoners, Cairns testifying in court, and Robertson handing a ticket to a woman driver on Andrew Street South.)

The force keeps the peace in a town of nine churches, six restaurants, three schools, one bar, a hospital, three banks, two funeral homes and a fairground where, so it is claimed, they hold the second biggest rodeo in Canada on Labour Day weekend.

Their tools are six pairs of handcuffs, a radar speeding apparatus, a walkie-talkie, four blackjacks, four riot batons, a cruiser, four 38s (target practice once a month at the town dump), a sawed-off shotgun, radio communications with four other Huron County stations, and a pair of binoculars.

"And most important of all," Day added, "our pens and notebooks."

One fact that impressed me about the cop's job is that Exeter has 132 business premises with 467 doors to be checked. But there's more. A sampling of last year's action shows the department mailed 532 letters, issued 95 parking tickets, sold 400 bicycle licences, found the owners of most of the 57 lost-and-found articles, assisted in 61 money escorts, returned home the 18 persons reported missing, laid 168 traffic charges and issued 301 warnings, charged 46 persons with liquor offences, and investigated 42 dog complaints, 169 motor vehicle collisions, 53 thefts, 21 occurrences of willful damage, 12 of breaking and entering, nine frauds, and 21 drug incidents. The men drove the cruiser 20,267 miles, worked 659 hours overtime, and were off sick a total of four days.

When Day moved to Exeter, his family started keeping a career scrapbook. In red ink under the first item—the ad for a chief—it says: "Once a cop, always a cop."

Not always. Day told me he quit the London force in 1967 because "I'd been working so long among hoods, I was beginning to think everybody was one. I was sick of it. I'd stopped trusting."

For a year he went on the road for a distillery. "I started meeting ordinary people again," he said. "And I found out, of course, that most people aren't hoods. It was a good feeling.

"Then one night in Port Stanley I heard a burglar alarm and I just started running and feeling for my gun that wasn't there....I knew I had to get back into police work. Because, you know, for satisfaction in the job—there's *nothing* like it. Not in the whole world!

"Mind you," said Day, "I'm talking about a *real* policeman. The best part of his job is what you don't hear about—the people he helps. That's eight out of ten; the other two go to jail.

"It's working with people. When I retire, I'd like to get a small restaurant, just so I can go on meeting people."

Did he miss the pace of city life?

"I enjoy it more here," said Day. "You have closer contact and it's much more relaxing. Yet, as chief, I'm into everything: traffic, administration, identification, morality, detective work, and so on.

"In London, I could look in on the clubs. Here I've got to be more careful....That bugs me a little. I don't join anything either; that shows favouritism. In a small place you've also got to be much more PR conscious.

"People are so close-knit and bad news hangs on. They ask for advice. Fathers about sons, and so on. There's no time for that in a big place. Here, if a boy steals $20 we bring in the family, discuss it, bring in the doctor. In the city there's no talk. The kid is put away."

Day said drugs were a problem in Exeter, too.

"Parents make fighting it difficult," he said, "because they bury their heads in the sand and say, 'My kid wouldn't!' But they do. And the parents should find out and help us. We're not out to prosecute teenagers. We're after the pushers.

"I understand, though, why people don't help the police more. They don't want to get involved, and I can't blame them. They're made fools of in courts by smart lawyers. Ordinary nice people who just want to do the right thing."

One week after he became police chief, Day had attacked double-parking on Main Street. At first people resented it; nobody had bothered before. "I told the fellas," Day recalled, "'Even if it's your next door neighbour—keep writing the ticket. They'll respect you for it.' In six months it wasn't a problem any more."

But traffic remains one of Day's major headaches. "In a small place," he said, "people are just more careless....The day the lights went up at Main and Sanders streets, three old men were watching. One of them said: 'Chief, I never thought I'd live to see traffic lights in Exeter!' They watched them blink that whole afternoon. And when they finally left, they walked right through the red."

———————

The third interruption in the three hours occurred then. A dapper man in a blazer rushed in, disturbed that the town-hall flag wasn't at half-mast because of the death of the Duke of Windsor. "Are you a bunch of Trudeauites?" he demanded.

Day promised he'd look into it right away. When the man left, Chief Day gave his chuckle.

The next morning I was out early with Constable McIntyre in the pale-blue cruiser through mist and gorgeous farmland to pick up the prisoners in Walkerton.

McIntyre is big—five feet 11 1/2 inches, 260 pounds. "I inherited all this honestly....My grandfather was six-four and weighed 340." He also told me he owned a few acres and cows and really always wanted to be a farmer. He talked with feeling about land, warm rain, cattle, and "corn you can almost see grow."

Like Day, a former first-class detective in London, he was glad he'd moved to Exeter. "They treat you as a person," he said.

There was wire-mesh guard between the cruiser's front and back seats, and the rear doors had no handles. The prisoners, both men in their early 20s with records, sat handcuffed to each other. The Indian never spoke, smiling "no" at offered cigarettes. The white man said: "We'll get a trial, and get it over with. We were intoxicated, you know, severely intoxicated."

When we got to the station, they were locked in the cells till their case came up. The white man said, smiling: "Jails here are fine. Better than Manitoba."

Court was in Exeter's Legion hall with Judge Glenn Hays, white-haired and frail, presiding.

The first case was an indecent assault on a 14-year-old girl involving late-night card playing and falling-down drunkenness. The defendant was a short, deeply tanned, toothless, middle-aged bachelor. He got 60 days. The second case concerned five burly teenagers who had beaten up a sixth in the men's room at a high-school dance. The biggest of the five, a huge kid, had finally jumped on the plaintiff and bitten him four times on the back.

"Did a doctor tend those wounds?" asked the judge.

"No sir," said the boy, colouring. "My Mum fixed me up."

There were snickers from the defendants. Chief Day reached the nearest in three strides and jabbed a hard, straight finger in his ribs. "Wipe the smirk!" he snarled.

That was the second time he came close to making that specific gesture I was waiting for.

In a whispered aside, Day guessed 90 days for the biter. But then, at the judge's request, the prosecutor had a few quiet words with him and told the court that the chief had said the defendant was employed, was a nuisance and menace when drunk but OK when sober.

"That has just saved your skin," said the judge and fined him $200.

The Winnipeg men came last. The Indian pleaded not guilty, saying he had just been out looking for his friend the night of the break-in. His case was dismissed. The white man pleaded guilty. He had a wife eight months pregnant, he said, and got 30 days. With good behaviour, he would serve perhaps 22.

Policemen, counsellors, the judge, the court stenographer, defendants, plaintiffs, and onlookers milled about in a kitchen next to the hall where many had left their raincoats.

Judge Hays chatted with the Indian.

"Going back to Winnipeg?" he asked.

"Yes," said the Indian.

"Hitchhiking?"

"Yes."

"Well," said the judge, "it's the right season for it."

One time when we were cruising around, Day said: "There are no prostitutes in Exeter, just a few 'free ladies.'

"There's a kid on LSD," he said, pointing. "And that's one of our three doctors."

The observations flowed on as we slowly rolled through quiet, shady streets.

"The town's sign painter is blind....Look at him slow down 'cause I'm behind him! The high school. That's George. There's the new bank. That fella once owned a roofing company. There was this old lady who made a left on the red. 'They told me it was all right,' she said. I said: '*They* are wrong! Don't you do it again— ever.' The Lawn Bowling Club....We might sell 500 bike licences this year. Made Ann Street a one-way to the hospital. A lot of motorcycle guys are bad. I guess it's their bag. We've had two suicides. Very few attempts....There've been no murders. Hotel's bar has been open since December, but only two calls for drunken violence. Turnips coming up nicely there...."

Once he stopped under a big tree and told what happened during the three-day snowstorm two winters ago. No traffic for 48 hours, hundreds stranded, hydro out, chill factor of 40 below, 12-foot high drifts, farmers dumping milk, a truck full of turkeys frozen to death. But then an army of 60 snowmobilers reported for duty! They delivered food, medicine, oil burners, and cattle feed; took doctors out on calls; checked abandoned cars; and fanned out across town combing every street and alley. In a way, it had been a good time for Exeter.

On my last night, a friend provided Chief Day with tickets for the races in London. Neither of us had been to a track in ten years and couldn't even decipher the program. But we hit on a fairly good system: ignore the Trackman's Selection and all tips. Go for nice names or low earnings; one man should place bets, the other cash them. And, during the race, one must concentrate on the horse, the other on the driver. We walked away with a $100 profit, not counting drinks.

Stopping at one or two London places on the way home, Day met several colleagues from the old days.

They didn't know who I was. When Day left the table a moment, one said: "The day Ted quit was like taking a cornerstone out of the station."

And another, an 18-year veteran with the London force: "He's the most competent, efficient, and nicest cop I know."

But the next day, moving a last time through Exeter's sleepy streets, with departure minutes away, I still hadn't seen Chief Day in real action.

Wobbling along on their bikes, the two young girls in hot pants talked and giggled and stayed oblivious to the car behind them. They were ten or 11 years old. They were so far on the street's left side, our car could have passed on the right. But it didn't. It merely crept closer. There was no other traffic. At least one minute went by. Then the car swerved right, leapt abreast the bikes, braked to stop, and Chief Day leaned out and roared:

"You kids want to get run over?"

The girls turned, braked, and slowly stepped down. They gave the chief a long, unsmiling look, and got the same in return.

Then, taking their time, heads high, they wheeled their bikes past the cruiser, across the front of it, climbed back on and pedalled away, backs straight. We didn't get even the littlest look when we passed.

Chief Day had finally done it, though.

Ninety Years Ago...

One of Exeter's first law enforcement officers was James Creech who served as Chief Constable and Street Commissioner from the early 1880s until 1900. A list of Creech's responsibilities, at a salary of $325 a year, included the following:

1. Patrol streets until midnight.
2. Clean the town hall.
3. Perform duties of sanitary inspector.
4. Enforce village bylaws.
5. Ring the town bell at 6 AM, 7 AM, 12 noon, 1 PM, 6 PM, 7 PM, and 9 PM. Curfew if required by council.
6. Collect Statute Labour commutations.
7. Light the street lamps.

Creech also had to deal with drunkenness, Sabbath breaking, dogs and cows on the loose, and "loafers on the streets making rude remarks to ladies."

Source: High-school principal Joe Wooden's to-be-published history of Exeter. [Published in 1973.]

Chapter 20

At the Snuff of a Candle, Dracula Appears

Around midnight, when wolves howl and bats careen along hallways, that polished and distinguished fiend from Transylvania, Count Dracula, likes to sip blood from the throats of young females. It's just one of his little ways; we all know about that. But there's something else the count needs. And most people do not know about that. He can, if need be, get by without it, but not as well, not as *effectively*....More about the count later.

We have first to move to Thunder Bay, Ontario, high up on Lake Superior, and there enter a dilapidated red-brick building. Some say it used to be an ordinary rooming house. But others report that women pleased sailors there once and that the ghost of the madam still wanders about the cobwebbed halls upstairs. She is a contented madam: a full house always pleased her. And this past summer [1973], and the one before that, her old place on Pearl and Water streets was packing 'em in.

The square inelegant structure is by the waterfront, right across from the railroad tracks. The walls shuddered when trains passed and trains passed often. But who cared? Toward 8 PM, night after warm night, Thunder Bayers and tourists crammed into that building. Excessive heat didn't stop them, nor rain, which leaked through the roof. They came, these people, adults and children alike, to have a good time—as did the sailors—but a different sort of good time. A couple of hours of the kind of pleasure that, years ago, people in towns and cities had all over this country—now it is very rare. A time to let old inhibitions go fly a kite! A time to see, oh Lord, the most devilish wickedness perpetrated! But then, thank goodness, always and inevitably, to witness virtue triumph and shy love blossom in a back-bending embrace. A time to hiss, cheer, boo, whistle, growl, squeal, and stand up and throw candy wrappers. Because for a couple of hundred performances 15 young actors and actresses did their utmost to rend the people's hearts. They acted bombastic fathers, suffering mothers, moustachioed villains, French maids, lunatics, innocent farm girls, brave lieutenants and, of course, in all his chilling magnificence, Dracula.

There are two big signs on 56 Water Street. One says Gay Nineties Theatre, the other Moonlight Melodrama. And melodrama is what is served inside: murdering, stealing, weeping, singing, fainting, loving, sword fighting, torturing, flirting and yes, *of course*, somebody gets tied to the railroad tracks! Most of the Moonlighters either attended or were graduates of the professional theatre program of Thunder Bay's Confederation College. In 1972, a group of them decided they wanted to spend their summer usefully and creatively. The city let them have the old house, which is in an urban renewal area and certain to be demolished by next year. They fixed the downstairs interior to give the mood of the Nineties. Red Victorian swag curtains in front of the windows, old-fashioned wallpaper, old posters, and even a picture of the old Queen, her eyes not approving at all. The foyer holds a long oak bar where, during intermission, pink and purple lemonade is sold, and cracker jack and candies from big glass bottles, two for one cent. Materials and furniture were scrounged from all over town. A massive, crank-up cash register on the bar, for instance, is on loan from a jewellery store where somebody's mother works.

They built washrooms and knocked out walls to create the 200-seat theatre. Around the walls of the theatre are seven candle-holders. The stage is small and rickety; the narrow dark passages behind barely leave room for the necessary rapid movement of actors and props.

But it all worked. It worked because of audacity, enthusiasm, talent, hard work and also, perhaps, because the whole group is a little crazy. They started with nothing that first summer and ended—highly successful; standing room only—$2,500 in the hole. Last summer they got an Opportunities for Youth grant of

$16,800. Thunder Bay gave $850—not an overwhelming sum—
and there were some small, private donations. Estimated working
budget for the season—including box office and bar receipts—was
about $40,000.

The performers drew a salary of $90 a week. But acting was only
part of the job. There were "details" like these to tend to: costumes,
props, backdrops, running the box office and the bar, publicity,
lights, musical arrangements, rehearsal schedules, sound effects, etc.,
etc. When I was there last August, I figured every cast member was
responsible for at least three jobs besides his or her roles.

There's no such thing, of course, as a "small" detail in a stage
production. A missing wig, a broken spotlight, or an umbrella
stand misplaced on stage can spell disaster. Ever see a curtain fall a
split second too soon? Or a dandy with a rip in his pants? Or a
pistol that doesn't go bang? At rehearsal it's hilarious. But with an
audience out there, not quite perceivable behind the lights, but oh
so ferocious, it's the purest sort of misery. On stage, things are
never, never supposed to go wrong accidentally.

And maybe this is especially so with melodrama. It's intended
to be fun and pretends to no more. But it is orchestrated fun. The
grand gestures, loud voices, exaggerated diction, horrendously
typical characters, incredible plot twists, interminable explanations
of emotions—all that is carefully paced and has a definite rhythm.
The tension that mounts and mounts until finally, finally the hero
leaps from stage-left in the third act and gives the blackguard his
what-for—that takes a lot of discipline and a lot of rehearsal. All of
it is fun and the audience is entertained—indeed, with the hissing
and cheering, entertains itself—but the cast must never once cease
to take themselves seriously. Apparently the cardinal rule is: self-
conscious burlesque is fatal.

The pleasure of melodrama, for actors and audience alike, is the
giving and taking on both sides. They stimulate one another. The
wilder the spectators' response to stage action, the better. It's the
same intense delight a good Punch & Judy Show provides. It's
participatory entertainment. And it's a pity there's so little of it
these days.

Theresa Castonguay, 20, who has been acting since her early
teens and is also the public relations director, said:

"I think what we do brings out a lot of good in people. Most of them want to be entertained. And that's what we do—entertain! A lot of movies and theatres tend to forget about that."

There's so little melodrama in this country, in fact, that artistic director William Pendergrast couldn't find a good Canadian melodrama when he wanted to add one to last summer's repertoire. Pendergrast, 48, a drama instructor at Confederation College, therefore wrote one himself. He wrote with each member of his group in mind. *The Secret of the Spyglass*, set in Kingston in the 1920s, had its world première in Thunder Bay two days after I left. Dignitaries, some in period costumes, were transported to the theatre in antique cars. The press had nothing but good to say about it, and, apparently, it became the public favourite. Now the repertoire includes such formidable competition as *Dirty Work at the Crossroads,* which some people went to see 12 times, *Only an Orphan Girl, The Last Loaf,* and, yes, *Dracula*!

Moonlight's two seasons have so encouraged Pendergrast and some of the cast that they plan a third one next year. It has, incidentally, become one of Thunder Bay's major tourist attractions. But the playwright-director has ambitions beyond that. He hopes to form a second company and take it across Canada next year playing 16 or so medium-sized cities en route.

"Too many people have said and written, 'Keep it going!'" he told me. "If it worked in Thunder Bay, it should work anywhere!"

They were a handsome group, the Moonlighters, attractive and fit. They shared one dressing room a bit larger than a one-car garage. The light-ringed mirrors over the single long makeup table reflected a chaos of costumes, hands painting faces, bodies dressing and undressing. Less than half of them thought of acting as a career, yet with only one day off a week, their lives revolved entirely around the theatre. That week, there was pride among them. René Boyer, 22, company manager and a vicious villain, and Kim Hansen, 19, set designer and fine country bumpkin, had just flown back from Ottawa. At the International Amateur Film Festival there, the two had walked away with Best Documentary and Best Canadian Film awards.

They were a close-knit group, too. Of course, the outside world was there, but vaguely so. Grim reality was that there were only three more days before the opening of *Spyglass*; that only two-thirds of the costumes for it were ready; and that tonight there was nobody to create the storm during *Dirty Work*....I volunteered. "Get involved, you cringing cur!" I said to myself. "Do something, you cowardly rascal!" You pick up melodrama language quickly.

So, during rehearsal, I blew and growled into a mike to simulate a roaring storm. It sounded like somebody blowing and growling into a mike. But the Moonlighters were kind and let me work the spotlight during solo numbers. It wasn't hard. I got a little poke from technical expert Wendy Hogan, 20, switched on, and pointed. No problems. Only once did the beam tremble slightly and that was when J. Kathleen Mayotte, 20, sang the haunting "All That Glitters Is Not Gold." At show's end that night I was less in awe of my fellow artists.

Melodramas are often preceded by warm-ups, some banter, some songs, all in keeping with the mood of the times. Whoever isn't needed early on in the first act joins in.

"Join in!" said my colleagues. "We need another warm-up man." So, in a red bow tie, red vest, and top hat, I was suddenly facing glaring lights and the eyes of 200-odd strangers. We sang "Tavern in the Town," "Mountain Dew," "I've Been Working on the Railroad." Nice songs, songs I've heard 50,000 times, but I didn't know the words to any of them. I tapped my foot, bobbed my head, moved my mouth. But 200 sets of eyes knew I was moving my mouth peculiarly.

Director Pendergrast has thick grey hair, mild brown eyes, and is a gentle man.

"You looked a little terrified," he said.

Respect for the Moonlighters' talent and nerve returned to its proper level.

And then, Dracula. Aged 22, David Duffield conveys a mood of such creeping, dreadful evil to the title role, that people have been known to simply walk out. Tall and caped, eyes glittering, he has merely to slowly point a long, limp, white hand at someone, and kids up front scream, "No! No!" He is an ominous presence.

There's no "Mountain Dew" stuff before *Dracula*. The audience enters the theatre lit by just those seven candles. Greg Reid, 22, the musical director, plays slow weird music on an electric organ. People find their seats almost in the dark. There's very little conversation and most of that in whispers. Then a pale spotlight hits the face of an actress on the stage. She wears a long black gown; her eyeshadow is blood red. She waits for silence. And then she says one word, very coldly: "Dracula."

But no, the play doesn't begin then. It couldn't: the candles are still burning. And so a fellow enters from the rear of the theatre. He wears a black frock coat, vest, bow tie, top hat with a black veil hanging from the back. His face is without emotion, the eyes dark. He is a man of mystery. With measured steps, he walks to the first candle, lifts the glass hood, and with a brass snuffer kills the flame. He replaces the glass hood. He does not hurry. Then he moves to the next candle and it too dies. *Who is this man? Who is he?* Slowly, he makes his way around the audience, to the opposite wall, and snuffs the life out of each remaining candle. Then the theatre is in total darkness. The play can begin.

Three fast and vigorous acts of madness, anguish, howling, and unspeakable terror follow. Finally, mercifully, the stake pierces that foul heart and a bat the size of a bedsheet wings screeching over the petrified audience.

They file out quietly. In the darkened foyer, Dracula's casket, closed, is on display. Some of the cast dressed in black, stand behind it, eyes down, not speaking. Few people can resist taking a closer peek at the casket.... *Of course he's not in there!*

"Did you see him bite her in the neck?" whispers one boy to another. Casually, without really looking, he touches the casket with his toe.

"Yeah. Right in the neck!" says the other boy.

True enough, Dracula did. But could he have done so, and could he have committed all those other chilling deeds without his trusty Candle Snuffer?

I was Dracula's Candle Snuffer.

Chapter 21

A Man in the Middle of Misery

CAMP BANIPUR, WEST BENGAL, INDIA

"**A**bsurd" is what J. Banerji called it. And maybe he was right: He's an old man and knows the world. Spend the night in one of his refugee camps? Absurd. No proper food, water, bathroom, or sleeping facilities. Also, there was sometimes violence in the camps. Kindly Banerji, retired inspector general of forests with the Indian government, thought it was a bad idea. He was in charge of, among others, Banipur, a camp holding 18,000 refugees from East Pakistan [in 1971; now Bangladesh]. He would find us a room in some nice home nearby. Yes?

The rickety little taxi fought Calcutta's insane traffic. Camp Banipur was only 31 miles northeast of the city, but it would take three hours to get there. The temperature was 98.3 degrees, the humidity 100 percent. Banerji wasn't happy. Sitting in back with him, Raymond Cournoyer was sympathetic: shaking his head the way people do there, meaning "No" to us but "Yes" to them, murmuring "*Acha, acha*" ("Yes, I agree, I understand, quite so.")

"You're right, food is important," he told Banerji. "If I give you some rupees, will you buy us fruit? Mangoes? You're such a good bargainer!"

And in fluent Bengali—learned during seven years as a teacher in East Pakistan (or East Bengal)—he told the driver to stop at the next market.

Banerji sighed. But at the market he took the rupees and went shopping. Raymond has a way with people.

We were surrounded almost the instant the car was parked. Maybe a dozen of them, whining kids in rags, thin, oily with dirt. They exuded a nasty, sweet smell. One of them had no hands and shoved his stumps through the back window—"No papa, no mama, no food!" Another's right leg was all twisted. A third had no legs at all and moved on a board on four roller-skate wheels. A fourth had no nose, just a hole. A fifth was hunchbacked. A cross-eyed sixth missed a foot and an arm. Hideous creatures, unbearable to look at. Give to one, you had to give to all. And then 50 more would probably swarm around. If you didn't give to those as well, they might get *mad*....

Raymond looked at them with interest. Their whining grew more insistent. The sun beat down on the cab's metal roof. Raymond has round cheeks and a sizable stomach. He was born in Magog, Quebec, 39 years ago. He is the field director in that part of India for the relief agency Oxfam.

His eyes moved from one little monster to the next. Then he leaned forward and took in his hand one of the stumps sticking through the window. He shook it and asked the boy a question. The kid promptly quit wailing. And one by one, so did the others. Raymond kept looking at the boy and holding his stump. The kid stared back, until one of the others poked him and he answered—one word. Raymond started slowly to smile; the smile grew; it pushed up his cheeks so the eyes narrowed to slits. He took the stump in both hands and massaged it back and forth. "*Acha*," he said, and shook his head in that odd way. "*Acha, acha*." The boy grinned first, then giggled. Behind him, the others took it up, looking at each other, looking at Raymond, pressing closer to his window, now entirely ignoring the driver and me. Raymond threw a question at another kid, and at another, but never let go of the stump. The replies came rapidly in cackly voices. Sweat ran out of Raymond's hair and down his face—"*Acha, acha, acha*." People stopped to watch. Something was happening. That chubby man was doing *something* strange. Because for a few minutes, that clutch of noisy garbage-eaters, surely the world's toughest experts at survival, were just children.

"I would like to work with boys like that," Raymond said later on, on our way again with Banerji and a basket of mangoes, bananas, and plums. "There's a priest in Bombay who does it. When all this is over, I would like to do it."

"All this" is seven-million-odd refugees from East Pakistan who have fled into India since, on 25 March 1971, Pakistan's military dictatorship in West Pakistan let loose a reign of terror there. "Over" means when the millions can safely return home. Right now the Indian government, with the help of Oxfam and other charity organizations, is working day and night just to feed, shelter, and give medical help to the refugees. Meanwhile, more of them keep coming as torrential monsoon rains make life ever more hazardous in the camps. Meanwhile, also, the world community's response to the disaster—for which there is no precedent—continues to be minimal. Material aid has come in relative dribbles, including Canada's contribution. And, at time of writing, no real effective political or economic action had been taken to stop the Pakistan army's organized butchery—of which the millions of fearful runaways are living proof.

Raymond and I planned to spend time in Banipur—one of the camps supplied by Oxfam—mostly so I could get some notion of day-to-day camp life. I had seen a number of other camps, but the visits had always been too short and hurried. Yet even now, when my visit would be 16 hours, I already regretted it couldn't be longer. It seemed pretty presumptuous to suppose one could penetrate, even a little, the life of an 18,000-soul community that quickly.

Banipur looked much like other camps, no better, no worse. Long, tarpaulin-covered sheds, many with open fronts and sides, jammed with human beings. The same queues for food, medicine, toilets, and pumps. The same incredible number of flies. The same slimy filth in ditches. The same worried, or afraid, or dull eyes. The same sores on bodies of children. The same stench. The same mood of boredom, especially among men—giving them work meant taking it away from local people who didn't have enough themselves. Women, at least, always had their families to care for. Children tried to play, but what and how in all that press of people?

Some 125 marvelously enthusiastic young Indian volunteers ran Banipur, distributing food, medicine, doing sanitation chores, etc.

For the medical team it was near quitting time—5:15 PM—when we got in, so I only had a few minutes with them. One young doctor, two third-year medical students, three nurses, and a compounder (drug dispenser), the team had treated 600 patients that day. In the dark old schoolhouse that served as dispensary and clinic, the doctor said some of the most common diseases were amebic dysentery, diarrhea, conjunctivitis, influenza, malnutrition, acidity, scabies, worms, measles, arthritis, eye diseases due to vitamin A deficiency, tuberculosis, otitis, rickets, asthma, diabetes, and respiratory diseases. He didn't mention cholera.

"It's the children that worry me the most," he said. "There are about 6,000 under the age of ten here. We haven't got a microscope," he added. "If we had just one, we could culture the stool of at least 50 people a day *here!* Now we have to send it to the city."

Around 7 PM, Raymond and I started a tour of the camp. Most of the Indian volunteers had left, as had a still worried Banerji; he had insisted that at least we should sleep between stone walls in the dispensary. We both wore *longis*, an ankle-length skirt-type garment men wear, made of thin cotton and infinitely cooler than trousers.

It must have taken a solid minute before we had our first 25 followers—children and a few men. Raymond strode on, sandals flapping. He pointed to an overflowing ditch, a row of latrines, a small naked girl, all alone, bawling angrily. He paid no heed to the quiet, growing crowd around us. Onward—past women tending cooking fires, a line-up at a water pump, two old ladies, one busy delousing the other, past the long sheds where people got up to have a better look at us. Strangers never came there at night.

The air was loaded with moisture, and not a hint of wind. When Raymond moved his head a spray of sweat flew off. More and more bodies crowded around us. Nobody said anything, just watched us. When Raymond finally stopped, everybody did. A man near him carried a small girl with sores on her head. Raymond looked at the sores and asked a question. The man nodded. The girl dug her face into the man's neck. With one finger Raymond tickled her side. For moments she didn't move, then she wriggled, and very quickly twisted around to look and back again. The man grinned—his child was shy. Raymond bent and picked up a boy standing at his feet. Shouting something, he swung him high over his head and down again. The boy raised his arms for more. Raymond lifted him so their noses touched and shouted something else, something funny, because the boy screeched and around us people laughed, and suddenly the crowd wasn't quiet any more, but talking, moving, pressing closer, dark heads bobbing, eyes on Raymond, giggling, grinning—same damn thing as in Calcutta.

Raymond took a few steps and a couple of hundred feet did likewise. The centre of the mass, he seemed to control it. A kind of electricity was working. His hands moved fast, so fast he seemed to touch a dozen people at once—poking, pressing, pinching, patting. He talked, listened, questioned, told jokes. His face was never still, smiling, frowning, cheeks rising and settling back. "*Acha, acha, acha.*" It lasted nearly three hours. In his long, white skirt, arms outstretched, sweating Raymond looked like a man from another time.

This is what he'd said a few days before: "There'll always be a place in the world where I can love people and people will love me."

A small man in khaki shorts came up and said something. Raymond shook a vigorous "*Acha.*"

"He asks us to have tea in his home," he said.

What home? *What* tea? This was a refugee lucky to be alive!

We slipped off our sandals before entering his shed. He spread a plastic sheet on the floor of hardened mud and lit an oil wick. The heat under the tarpaulin seemed twice as bad as outside. The wife, a frail, pretty woman, squatted ignored in a corner. Once or twice I heard her chuckle. Our host introduced each of his ten children, eight of them boys. The family's living space wasn't much larger than a double bed. Our host's name was Onil Krisna Debanot. His house and store had been burned by the soldiers about a month ago, he said. From a cloth purse he fished a few coins; there were enough left to make up maybe one rupee. A rupee is roughly one-seventh of a dollar.

The coins were handed to someone in the mass of people behind us. The tea would be purchased in an Indian shop outside the camp.

Not only three glasses of hot sweet tea were handed through the crowd to our host, but biscuits as well. He served us casually—tea with guests in one's home was not a big deal. I followed Raymond's example and did not speak thanks.

Debanot told of a doctor at home who had poisoned himself because he was so afraid. He held his hand half an inch above the head of his oldest son, 14, and said bullets had passed *that* close there. He was worried, he said, and had no peace of mind. Yes, he wanted badly to go home, but wouldn't until he was sure it was safe.

Back in the dispensary, we sat down at a table with a candle stuck in an empty can of sulphadiazine tablets. We had a meal of mangoes, bananas, and plums.

The night's dominant sound was crickets. Millions going full blast. Outside, and inside too, things flew through the air. Flies had no thought of retiring, mosquitoes were just getting up. And other things scurried unseen across the floor, whispers racing from corner to corner.

There was a knock on the door and two young men came in carrying some books. They were students, they said, both 20 years old. Watching Raymond earlier they had felt that, well they just had to talk to him.

"*Acha.*"

The books, printed in Bengali, held stories and songs. But there was one special song....Was it all right if one of them sang it?

"*Acha.*"

The boy had black curly hair and a very thin moustache. He sang with all his might, neck veins swelling. On the wall the shadow of his head swayed along. Here's a crude translation:

> Why is not your soul concerned with God?
> Because if you believe in God after death,
> God will give you happiness.
> The one who can listen to the voice of his soul will find the link with God.
> It's only after death that you understand the love of your mother.
> In that same way you will understand the love of God.
> At the moment of your death your mother will cry—but she will soon forget.
> After your death your ashes will be kept in an urn—but it is very little.

Wealth makes people love you, but it is a joke—after death you
will not have it.
But he who believed in God—God will help him.

The two discussed the books with Raymond for nearly an hour.
We offered cigarettes, but they said no; we should smoke their
homemades. I hadn't been able to join in the talk much, yet their
last words were for me.

"When you learn Bengali," said the singer, "I will give you a
book that will make you cry."

Afterwards, Raymond said:

"It is bloody terrible how these people must live in the camps.
Soon they won't be human beings anymore. But some say: 'There
are too many in the world anyway—a million dead is maybe a good
thing.'"

He was getting groggy with fatigue. The next few things were
bits of though spoken out loud:

"If we could simply start *dialogues*—India and the foreign
world, Canada and Quebec. The 'other one' is not worse, not
better—just *different.* We're always stuck with *pettiness.* There's
no leadership, no cause. How big, how bloody *big* men could be!"

He stumbled to a wooden bench and spread his sleeping bag.
He warned me he snored. And he did, the whole night through.

The camp had grown quiet, with only pockets of low talk. I
could see no more than a half-dozen lights from oil wicks. Then
the night was shattered by screaming and the sound of flesh beating
flesh. It went on and on and then abruptly stopped. The crickets
took over again until three male voices started yelling and I heard
slaps. They, too, kept at it for a while. Then a woman started
weeping....

Around midnight it drizzled briefly. Afterward the heat seemed
worse. The eruptions of loud voices and sometimes violence
continued. Out there 18,000 people were packed together.

The rain came a little after 2 AM. It choked all other sound. Its
beat on the tarpaulin roofs must have been terrific. It plunged
down with a force all living things had to fear. There was nothing
cozy about it, nothing friendly. I didn't know it could rain
like that. And I didn't know *that* rain—it lasted no more than

30 minutes—was the season's first; that in some camps—not Banipur *then*—refugees next morning would squat ankle-deep *inside* their shelters; that the drift of human excrement from ditch to path to living quarters had already begun; that experts predicted that only now the dying would begin in earnest.

Dawn broke around 4:30. In the gray light, a dog chased a small bird skipping ahead. But he gave up because the mud was too deep. An old man went into a fit of coughing. A child started crying, and others joined in. Men took little walks, hawking, and spitting. Women lit fires that just smoked. It began to drizzle.

Raymond awoke grumpily, didn't like the looks of the world, and went back to sleep.

Later, we took another walk around the camp. It happened as before—Raymond worked magic again.

Around 8, the first Indian volunteers arrived bringing bad news. The previous night a state politician had been assassinated in Calcutta. His party had called for a *bandh* in the city from 4 AM to 4 PM that day. That meant that this city holding millions (guesses range from eight to 12 million) would come to a complete standstill. No traffic of any kind; all shops closed. Ignoring the strike was to risk death.

Bad news. Now we'd be stranded in Banipur all day. Oxfam's jeep couldn't travel either. Sixteen hours earlier I had truly wanted a longer stay. Here was a gift of more hours…but I was tired of the stink, mud, flies, sweat, filth, grief, pain, and misery.

Raymond's reaction was different: "*Acha.*"

So we tramped around some more. Food distribution started— milk for the kids—and Raymond jumped in reorganizing line-ups. He was also turning them on again.

I was thinking that I had seen scenes like that for what seemed like years, when something soft and sticky stole into my hand. I looked down and there was this solemn, skinny little kid. We looked at each other, and after a bit we smiled. I had to take some pictures, and I guess I forgot him. But as soon as my hand was free, he took it again. In the next two hours he wandered away only once, to urinate behind a shed. Raymond was busy, so somebody else helped me find out at least his name and age—Monoranjan Nath, eight. God knows what has happened to him.

About 10 AM, the medical team and Banerji drove up in the Oxfam jeep. Good news: vehicles with red crosses on them were permitted on Calcutta's streets. The jeep had a red cross.

There were no goodbyes to say, except to Monoranjan. And him I couldn't talk to. So I took his picture, which I think he enjoyed. And I gave him a kiss, which I think he didn't enjoy.

Leaving Banipur, the jeep's wheels churning through the mud, I was thinking of my cool hotel room, a long bath, fresh clothes, and cold beer.

I didn't want to think about anything else.

The Story of a Reticent Canadian

Raymond Cournoyer loves to talk, but not a lot about himself. For instance, this may be the closest he'll come to explaining why he's doing what he does: "I'm very concerned with the condition of men." It isn't modesty so much as that he's simply too intensely preoccupied with what's going on around him, with *other* people. Even these bits of biographical data were a chore to extract:

Born: Magog, Quebec, 1931; BA degree, St Joseph's University, New Brunswick; left for East Pakistan in 1958 and taught school there for seven years; returned to New Brunswick for further study in 1965; started working part-time for the relief agency Oxfam in 1966 while studying international development; in November, 1969, was appointed Oxfam's field director in eastern India and East Pakistan.

And that's where he is now.

Chapter 22

Travels Through a Winter Country

A strange assignment. Travel across Canada, but avoid the cities. City people are always being interviewed. Stick to the small centres, talk to the people who are seldom heard from. Ask them why they stay where they are, what they think of this country. In other words, there is a lot of country beyond the urban and suburban sprawl of Montreal or Halifax or Toronto or Vancouver or Winnipeg. A lot of people, too.

Then, do it in winter. Most "cross-Canada" efforts are done in summer. More scenic. The winter makes a oneness of Canada. A white oneness, for the most part. Except for maybe the West Coast. Also, winter is Canada. We have more of it than any other season.

So that was it. Canada in the winter. Canada as seen through the eyes of people who are seldom asked what they think of Canada because the people of Toronto and Montreal are always talking about the subject and nobody else can be heard. At least, not very often.

Actually, as I sat in my plane at Montreal airport one night in early February [1972] waiting to make the first step—out to Vancouver and then back by easy stages to the Atlantic provinces—the feeling that this was a strange assignment subsided. Instead, I began to think that I was lucky.

Because how many people, really, have this kind of an opportunity to find out even a small bit about the practically unknown Canada?

Next to me sat a stocky young man with a round, friendly face who had his arm around a sleepy boy, about five, in the window seat. His name was Eddie Stang, he said, and he was going home to Calgary. That was the wife across the aisle—a quiet, pretty woman holding a little girl's hand. An assistant production manager, he had spent a month at his firm's Montreal plant. It had been interesting and so on, but he wasn't sorry to leave. They had lived in an apartment.

"It was like a jail," said Eddie. "At home we have a birdhouse in the yard. Where are you going to put a birdhouse on Decarie Boulevard?"

My turn then—name, destination, job, and a bit about the trip. But why in winter, Eddie wanted to know, and why avoid big towns? I told him why and he seemed to like the sound of it.

"You know," he volunteered, "I was raised in a small place...."

The journey had begun.

Eddie told me of his late grandfather, Peter Stang. A Russian of German descent, Peter came in 1909 to homestead in the bleak, flat country near Macklin, Saskatchewan, about 140 miles west of Saskatoon. He married twice and had 25 children. On 1 January 1971, according to the third edition of Peter's family tree, his "tribe" numbered 748. Last July, the Stangs had a family gathering near Macklin. About 500 showed up and they had to wear name tags.

"We're as Canadian as you can get," Eddie boasted, and he listed some of the nationalities in his family: Irish, Scottish, Ukrainian, Russian, French, Japanese, Dutch, Indian, German, Italian, British, and Norwegian. "We're all over the country, but there are still a lot of us up in Macklin," he said. "You've got to visit it."

Eddie, 30, referred again and again to his father, also called Peter. "You've got to meet him," he said. "Last year, Dad raised $700 walking 27 miles in one of those miles-for-millions deals. He's 69. We had a plaque made for him."

Eddie has 15 brothers and sisters. However, after his mother died, his father remarried last August and the bride had 13 of her own—so that made 29.

He said he missed the country in Calgary. So, whenever they could, he and his family went camping in the mountains, or visiting relatives on farms. "You say hello to your neighbour in the country," he said. "And you're not always thinking about locking doors."

He grew thoughtful: "We've got freedom in this country. More than anywhere else. But there's a lot that's wrong." And with conviction: "We've got to get back to family life. Things are happening too quickly. This country is growing too fast. I'd like to see the trend reverse. Success isn't money. A good home-time life is what counts!

"Leaving the kids a house, or a car, or money, doesn't mean anything!" said Eddie. "The only real thing you can hand down is the environment—and we're hard at work ruining it. The people we're voting in aren't doing the job—look at the Great Lakes! We've got to keep what we have left. We've got to keep the world!"

An English poet said the reason you feel so disconnected after a long flight is because your soul can't travel that fast and needs time to catch up. Soulless, therefore, I sat in the Calgary bus next day, waiting to pull out of Vancouver's depot. It was noon under a cloudless sky and the temperature was 50°F (10°C). The thought of the thousands of miles of snow, ice, and wind ahead was a bit depressing.

The route was through Chilliwack, Hope, Merritt, Kamloops, Revelstoke, and Golden, my stop. Uniformly garish towns, all of them, like the others we passed through. Clumps of gas stations, motels, and chicken palaces sprawling in valleys amid perhaps the most awesomely beautiful country in the world. A British-Columbia friend had explained that the towns are all ugly because it's still pioneer country. Whatever, they mess up the mountains. But there weren't many of them; mostly it was mountains with immense slabs of snow bracing their sides, water rushing down black rocks, thousands of still trees, and frozen lakes. When dark fell, those colossi turned into menacing shadows, but a thin slice of moon kept an eye on them.

Behind me in the bus, a blue-haired, elderly woman from Burnaby remarked on that moon to a thin, quiet young woman from Vancouver. The blue-haired woman had remarked on *everything*, and in a voice that cut through all talk, thought, and sleep. There's a voice like it on every bus. She was special, however; I timed her and she kept it up for nearly six hours and 30 minutes. On and on she rattled in short, breathless sentences, with lots of "she saids" and "I saids," and an occasional "bloody" or "damn." Like the "bloody" Beatles had ruined our youth, the "damn" foreign restaurants were wrecking Vancouver. On and on, about Johnny Cash, false teeth, a daughter in Seattle, phone-in shows, sex, neighbours, drapes, children, cancer, dope, money, fortune-telling, a straying son-in-law, her late husband's split personality, ice cream, the weather, buttons...until she got off in Kamloops around 8 PM, an old woman, alone, with a nervous walk.

Behind me, the timid young woman, who got the brunt of it, heaved a sigh. We both had a cigarette as the bus rolled on through the dark.

Donna Merrett, thin, brown-eyed, 27 years old, and the mother of two, wasn't really that timid. It was just that the old woman was an old woman, and what could you do? Donna told me that she had once gone to school with Nancy Greene, and two years ago she had a spinal fusion that nearly crippled her for life. Before getting married and moving to Vancouver, she had driven a cab in Golden, her hometown, and even guided construction workers into the bush. Now she was going to visit her parents.

Her father was a foreman in the Kicking Horse sawmill and also owned a 60-acre trailer park three miles outside town. He had bought it for $18,000 and last week was offered $60,000. She talked with feeling about him. The happiest day of her life, she said, was when he started doing well.

Pierre Trudeau was another matter. "I don't like him," she said. "He's spent more money than all the prime ministers put together and he's done us not one iota of good. And look at the kids on welfare! He's not showing them responsibility!"

She drew an orange plastic wallet out of her purse and showed me pictures of her husband, children, and parents.

Back on politics, Donna said: "I wish Diefenbaker was 40 years younger. He was doing the job. Now when he says something, everybody laughs and calls him a stupid fool."

Her husband worked in a sawmill in the city and they were also the caretakers in their apartment building. On vacations they went camping in the mountains. "*Home* is what this country is for me," she said. "I'm proud of it, admire it, love it, and enjoy it. I'd never live anywhere else."

Donna would tell a foreigner about Canada: "Go see it! You'll love it! Never mind the separatists—the Quebec or BC ones—they're fools. We've got to stick together, and that's what we're doing. Go see the Calgary Stampede, the Salmon Derby, the Klondike, and Victoria. It's a shame though you couldn't have come in the 50s—life was simple then."

If she was making my trip, she said, she would ask people: "Are you content with what you've got? Or are you going to keep this dog-eat-dog thing going? We're growing too fast. Shouldn't we be working for, well…harmony?"

Golden, I learned next morning from the motel's owner, had the largest per-capita Alcoholics Anonymous group in Canada. It also had a bookshop: Bridge Books, owned and operated by Mrs Chris Schiesser, a 70-year-old mother of eight. The next place you could buy a book was in Banff, 60 miles east.

A tiny, white-haired lady, Mrs Schiesser came to Canada from England 40 years ago. She was having soup and black-bread sandwiches in the back of the little white clapboard building with assistant Mike Sinclair, a blond six-footer from Vancouver. In other seasons, Mike liked to work in the bush, but in winter he preferred the bookshop because it was "nice and warm."

Mrs Schiesser said most of her stock was in paperbacks, 80 percent of it nonfiction—philosophy, psychology, nature guides, biographies, and histories of the West.

She has 18 grandchildren. She also sculpted in soapstone, but American tourists wouldn't buy her work because it wasn't genuine Eskimo—"I'm being discriminated against!"

A busy and committed lady, she was editing a book on Golden's history and she produced a weekly column, "Valley View-Point," for the *Golden Gazette*. That week's column protested the location of a $30-million development called Village Lake Louise in Banff National Park and urged readers to sign a petition to that effect at the Town Office or the store.

Mike changed the subject. "It takes five to ten years," he said, "for young people to get over the damage the present educational system does to them. But teachers and preachers are loosening up. I'm optimistic.

"There's tremendous introspection right now. We know industrialization is going much too rapidly, yet we're not watching, gauging, its effects enough.

"Let's get into it in Canada," he said. "Let's look to Eastern Philosophy for knowledge or to our own Indians."

After some coaxing Mrs Schiesser let me take her picture. But Mike wouldn't—"There are lots more worthwhile people."

Peter Palumpo, on the other hand, enjoyed being photographed. Owner of Golden Taxi Ltd—three cars and an old yellow school bus—he seemed to do most of the driving himself. He worked, he said, an average of 17 hours a day, seven days a week. But now he was turning over $5,500 a month and that might climb to $7,000. He was 40 years old, of Italian descent, and had five kids. It was a long time since he had taken his wife to the Legion.

Short, swarthy, unshaven, and fantastically energetic, Peter never seemed to stop—driving, talking, chewing gum, singing, and sucking his teeth. "Yeah, I hustle!" he admitted. "Man, I take pride in my work. I'm not in it so much for the money as...to make a man of myself! I sweep the cars and the bus. Keep 'em clean. Man's gotta take pride in his work. First himself, then his work.

"What's wrong in this country are the laws—they're confusing! The magistrates, lawyers, and Mounties twist 'em around. That's *all* that's wrong. We've got our Canada Pension Plan, BC medical plan, and we've got our freedom! And we don't need the Americans. I like them all right, but I don't like them coming here and taking over! The government should make sure always to keep 51 percent."

———— ⚬•❈•⚬ ————

As Eddie Stang, the one in the plane, had suggested, I looked up his father, Peter, when I got to Calgary. His small, snowed-under house was in the north end. The new Mrs Peter Stang, Mary, answered the door. In her strong face there were many lines that spoke of work and pain.

"Come in and welcome," she said slowly. "I just hope you won't harm us."

I assured her that I wouldn't and couldn't, but it hadn't been a question.

And then I was inside a house full of framed photographs. Photographs of old men and old women with kerchiefs around their heads, of young people in wedding dress, of children with stuck-down hair, of groups stiff at attention; photographs in barnyards, at dinner tables, and in front of cars. All photographs of Stangs.

Peter Stang, now retired, looked like his father, Peter, and his son, Eddie—stocky, round-faced. But Peter also had the most stubborn blue eyes I'd ever seen. I don't know if "stubborn" applies to eyes, but his were stubborn. Yes, we could talk, he didn't mind, but those eyes were watching, and if they didn't like what they saw conversation was absolutely guaranteed to die.

But it was OK. And Peter began to recall the old days. He'd come to Macklin when he was six. He remembered the first house of clay and straw amid 160 flat acres where nothing hid you from the wind; when it was a week's trip to go to town for supplies; when you never needed to lock your door because there was no stealing; when a man's word was holy; when, even in the hungry 30s, there was better talk and more laughing than now; when people worked so hard they didn't have time to get nervous; when everybody was poor, *understood* what it was like, and so helped one another; when people married once for always; when you put oats and water in your tires—four new ones cost $20.45!—and when you got home it was all porridge; when he sold a whole steer for $1.89 and then got docked because it wasn't dehorned; when he and his brothers made "Bennett burgers" for the neighbours; when people said every day, "It can't get worse"—but it did; when weddings went for three days and guests might consume 16 eight-gallon kegs of beer, 20 gallons of whisky, 25 gallons of wine, a steer, and a big fat pig.

"We're still," said Peter, "living in the best damn place in the world...but it's not going right. If all parties worked together in Ottawa, instead of fighting like children, maybe....Canada had the best damn opportunity to build up fast. Ideas from everywhere. Now we're ruining it fast.

"I'm afraid. This country is heading for revolution. We'll vote for the devil, like we did in Russia. It will be bloody! The czars didn't care for the working people, and they don't care here either. This country means everything to me. When the census man comes around I tell him: 'Came from Russia, born in Argentina, nationality German—*so I'm 100 percent Canadian!*'" Like his son, Peter listed the nationalities in his family, and then he shouted: "I'm related to the whole damn world!"

We had supper. Corn, mashed potatoes, fried chicken, gravy, sweet jelly, pickles, olives, and *Krepple*, a German pastry. Mary talked of the time she had a baby while out in a field on a binder. And she mentioned that Peter's first wife had been her bridesmaid when she married her late first husband.

"Why," Peter abruptly demanded, pointing at the full table, "does grain rot here, and over there people starve? That means there's something wrong in this world. Many things are wrong. Unemployment—a human being isn't happy unless he makes his own living. Education—TV could be so good for kids, but they put on shooting and killing and stealing. Young kids—I don't like the way they're being spoilt; school without end but no job. And if they go bad, who can blame them? It's the upbringing....I remember my father waited three days before spanking. He never touched us when he was mad."

Peter Stang gave one final insight: "All the hate in this country," he said, "doesn't come from people. It's the political stuff that spreads the hate."

———◆◆◆———

In the plane to Saskatoon, a woman in high red boots, returning from two weeks in Hawaii, said her town was lovely in spring, summer, and fall, but in winter "the closest thing to Siberia. Even when we go on a little car trip," she told me, "we carry candles, sleeping bags, hot coffee, and tinned heat. We're a hardy lot, but you can never tell in this country."

She was so right.

———◆◆◆———

The little blue rented car shot along the road in the white-on-white nothingness that is Saskatchewan in winter. The flat land was in its way as awesome as the mountains. Nothing moved except dry snow whipping low across the highway. In the distance, the overcast sky became indistinguishable from the land. The road plowed straight ahead, with hardly a bend, telephone poles running alongside, and for long minutes not a house, a vehicle, or even a fence in sight. It was like that most of the way from Saskatoon to Macklin (pop. 901) where the streets were solid ice and there was hardly a soul about.

I phoned Paul and Mary-Ann Fisher. (Mary-Ann is a Stang and had been told I was coming.) "Go six miles south out of town," she said, "three west, one north."

It was a trip over icy dirt roads through fields of snow. The Fishers were a friendly, gentle couple in early middle age with three children. They had always lived in the area and farmed 960 acres. I think they enjoyed having a visitor.

"We have an awful quiet life," said Paul. "Sometimes too quiet....There's not much work in winter. Just keep the roads open, care for the hogs. Two winters ago I got so bored—we didn't have the hogs then—I almost quit. But Mary-Ann said no."

"We stay because, well, we like farming," said Mary-Ann. "And it's the kids. There's no fear here of crime or being mugged. We know everybody 50 miles around."

"And what's money?" Paul said, rolling a cigarette. "It means nothing. As long as you eat, be a little happy, pay your taxes....You're freer, too, on the farm. There's very little bad gossip. Neighbours *need* each other. We do chores for each other. We don't phone before visiting. We make our own entertainment rather than go to some smoky bar full of bad language."

Paul picked up a wallet lying on a table. "I don't want to brag," he said, "but can you leave this lying around your city house? We *never* lock our doors. The only people who would come in would be lost or need help."

Paul said he found it difficult to describe being a Canadian. "You talk to one, and he's different," he said. "Then you talk to another and he's even more different. He's a free man. Works when he wants to work. He's an easy drinker. Main thing is, he's free; he can say what he *wants*."

"Trudeau has his good points, but he doesn't do much for us. Doesn't understand us. You can't until you live here. I used to like Dief, but now David Lewis is my man. We understand what he says. Smallwood and Dief are very alike when I think of it. The same thirst for glory...."

"I wouldn't care if the United States took us over. They already own a lot anyway. It might even be better for us."

Mary-Ann said supper was on. Afterwards, would I like to come along to a "carnival" in town?

Macklin's Biggest Little Fair was in an unheated indoor rink. The program had little kids in costumes doing bits of figure skating, and closed with a game between two all-girl hockey teams. The place was packed. In the crowd Mary-Ann confided: "Paul used to be so shy he had to take a drink when he came courting me." During intermission, they served hot dogs, pop and coffee. Paul introduced me to the show's emcee, high-school teacher John Feser, 38, a father of nine.

John kindly took off ten minutes. A thoughtful, articulate man, he spoke of many things.

"There's a challenge here to a way of life that people hold dear; a challenge of survival. A little community like this will have to fight to hang on. There's been a tremendous evacuation from here in the last ten years...

"Governments should keep the land productive, but also as a way of life. They're forgetting the staple producer. He's not getting taken care of properly. We've got to keep people here, even encourage them to leave cities and go back to the land.

"There's a genuineness here, a trueness, a kindness, a helpfulness.

"I'm afraid of the obsession with financial security in this country...the endless vacuum we seem to be heading into. I'm greatly worried by the growth ethos. And I'm worried about education. The system is basically obsolete, a 1940 system. We're gradually getting back to people, but it'll take at least ten years. We're going to have to educate for life, to cope with *life*, rather than machines.

"The people, I think, who are contributing the most to Canada right now are the social critics, the young, and the Indians."

Then he had to get back to his mike on the ice.

After the game the Fishers suggested I meet them the next morning, Sunday, at church.

The little wooden structure, all by itself on the flat white fields, was full to capacity. Yet it was six below with winds of at least 30 mph. On entering, I picked up a copy of a sort of weekly newsletter the priest puts out. It stipulated the week's Masses, who would lead the rosary, names of the church sweepers, time and place of a card party, etc. Item 12 said: "Did you know: that DAY CARE CENTRES is just another trend towards communism (raise the kids like cattle), and the work of the devil, to destroy MOTHER-HOOD and put enough men out of work by mothers working, so as to start a revolution."

The sermon dealt with two matters. We were urged to buy a new American edition of the Bible within the next two weeks for just $9. "It's beyond me," the elderly priest told his people, "how it can be so cheap!" And we were further asked to donate gener-ously to something called Peace Development. That was church that cold February Sunday.

———◆◆◆◆———

I drove another route back to Saskatoon, but it was hard to tell the difference. Same endless flatness and blowing snow.

There was a small bend ahead in the road about halfway between Kerrobert and Biggar, a distance of 60 miles. The road was as deserted as the land. The bend held a snowdrift, and I slowed down to 35. But there was a faint jolt, and suddenly I came to a dead stop eight yards off the road in a field. The field was covered in four or five feet of snow. The car stood half on its side, and snow covered the window on the driver's side. All one does then is shut off the motor and talk to oneself—not Paul Fisher's kind of language. Then one climbs out, looks around, and concludes that one is very badly stuck in the middle of nowhere. The wind started to hurt right away. There was no sound except that wind.

Minutes went by before the first car appeared. It stopped instantly. The two men in it tried pushing, but the car didn't budge. Then three guys in a pickup tried it with a rope, but it snapped. Only a tow truck could do it, they said, and one wasn't likely to come out on Sunday. Then I was alone again.

The next car dropped me at the silent hamlet of Springwater, four miles on. I knocked at the door of the only house at which there was a car parked. It was opened by an elderly man in a hat and overcoat.

Lucky I caught him, he said, because two minutes later he'd have been on his way to son Bill's farm for supper. As he ran the local switchboard, I wouldn't have been able to phone anyone till 30 minutes further. Sit down, he said, and he got busy cranking at his ancient board. Not a single garage would help—it was Sunday. Finally, a farmer with a big truck said he'd come.

It only took a minute to pull me out. The farmer, of course, wouldn't accept any payment.

Onwards, then, with caution. Ten miles further, and every red light on the dashboard started blinking. I stopped and great gusts of steam jumped from beneath the hood. Again I was stuck alone in that wind, worse now because the sun as going down.

The first Good Samaritan was as useless as I. Neither of us could even open the hood. The second did better and diagnosed the problem as a worn-out fan belt and something about a ripped generator pipe. No way could I drive further, he said. So he offered a slug of sweet smooth wine and we pushed that miserable thing off the road and drove on to Biggar.

I heard it at least five times that night: "New York is big. But this is BIGGAR, Saskatchewan!" But what impressed me was that Biggar's young Donald Rogers and his cousins Jim and Glen came out to tow the car in.

While they fixed it at the garage, we talked and had some whiskey in Styrofoam cups.

Donald, who had never been on a plane, train, or a bus, told me that the most beautiful thing he had ever seen in his 18 years were two deer standing in the sunset on Ed Easaw's farm at Meadow Lake in May, 1971.

"Doesn't matter where I go," he said. "I'd always come back to Canada. It's got everything...for everybody."

I asked the three a stock question: Name one or more Canadians, living or dead, who, in your opinion, have made the greatest contribution to Canada. They were like most people I met—when they really thought about it they couldn't come up with even one name. It isn't, apparently, an easy question in Canada.

———◆◆◆———

Flin Flon, Manitoba (pop. 13,000), was the furthest point north I got on the trip. Canada's map shows how very little north that is. But it's on a clear day in a plane above that bush and lake country that the incredible vastness of this land hits home. At least it did so to me on the three-hour flight up from Winnipeg.

On driving into Flin Flon, I had the sensation of entering a fort, a safe place in the wilderness, but one that also shuts in, locks up, and isolates.

I met George, a long-haired white man, and John, a long-haired Indian, in the bar of the Flin Flon Hotel by going over and asking if I might sit down with them. John said sure, as long as I paid for my own. Both were out of work and not very cheerful. Not at first, but we moved to a jammed beer hall that had live music and there John, a guitarist himself, felt better, especially when they played some of his favourites. I noted he was the only Indian. He and George were drinking their beer quickly.

"That's all there's to do," George shouted over the music.

"Yeah!" John agreed.

A bit later John said to me: "I'm as good as anybody—right?" That was all for a while until George leaned forward and emptied the contents of his shirt pocket onto the table—plastic bag of hash, cigarette papers, and three plastic tubes of different pills.

"Come to a party?" he shouted to his friend.

John looked at the items on the table and slowly nodded yes. He was getting drunk.

"You?" George shouted at me.

I nodded as well.

We went back to the Flin Flon Hotel then, John weaving several paces behind. A kid with a car was waiting there. John said he had to see somebody first, disappeared, and never came back. George, the kid, and I drove to the outskirts of town and stopped at a new, ranch-style home buried in snow. There were six other young guys inside drinking beer in the kitchen. It was hot and some of them had taken off their shirts. From the living room came the blast of rock.

Present were Pete, Bill, Mike, Ron, Tom, and Al. I didn't ask last names. They were all in their late teens. It was Mike's house; his parents were gone for a couple of days. Clearly, George was guest of honour: he had the stuff. They said girls were coming but none did. Pretty soon all talk ceased. The young men drank and passed smokes around. Some lay down on the floor. One of these, eyes glassy, said slowly and distinctly: "Every man has a movie of his past in his head that puts real films to irrelevant shame."

I left at 2 AM, but the party went on all night. They drank all the beer and smoked all George's hash. A few consumed some of the pills. He told me so next morning when I met him hanging around the lobby of the hotel.

"I've been to Winnipeg, to Toronto, but keep coming back here because my father is dying. Thinks he is anyway," he said in a tired voice. "I don't see much of him, but I know he likes me to be around. I also come back for the old memories. But there aren't many left...."

I had guessed George to be about 30. I asked him.

"Eighteen," he said.

———◆·◆·◆———

From the raw magnificence of the North to the civilized gentleness of southeastern Ontario. From Toronto along the lakeside awhile, then up along secondary roads to Perth, 40 miles southeast of Ottawa. Perth, for no better reason than that my mother was born there. There was snow there, too, but not like in Saskatchewan. "A soft white woollen blanket," fit.

Through one historic village after another, their architecture varied and distinct, with shop signs in Old English lettering. Farm homes and buildings, fences and trees, all showed the mark of care and pride. A shabby barn was almost a landmark.

Lunch in Perth's 150-year-old Imperial Hotel dining lounge; white linen, flowered English china, dark wood furniture, old copper pots holding real plants, brass sculptured plates on off-white walls, a massive grandfather clock in a corner, sunshine through small windows, a chubby blonde waitress, and excellent food.

Owner Eric Scrivens, who bought the place two years before, said he planned to renovate it. He was tearing down the painted plywood that was covering lovely fieldstone walls. He and his wife Marion, he said, did all the decorating and refurbishing.

A huge man, who used to be on the road for a brewery, Eric said he has really only one gripe: "The antiquated liquor laws in this country."

He introduced me to Fred Dixon, 28, who had dropped by for a sandwich. Fred Dixon and his group, "The Friday Afternoon," were the star attraction at the Imperial. Some of Fred's songs are "Last Fatal Duel," about the last duel in Canada, "Tom Thomson," about Tom Thomson, and one called "Jim's Used Car Lot." Records had been made of these, and he took me home and played them.

"I love working small towns," said Fred, "specially around here. People are very warm. I don't dig cities at all. Here I can drive seven miles, cut a hole in the ice, and catch a pickerel."

Before taking up music as a career, Fred worked five years with handicapped children. "I really enjoyed that," he said, "but finally it started to get to me."

I said I'd look in at the hotel that night and meanwhile went to visit Eddie Lambert, the former owner of the Imperial. The present owner suggested I see him because he was "as honest as the day is long."

Eddie, 68, was shovelling snow in front of his home across from the Catholic church. He said his main worry was the "changes in our values."

"How do we cope with them?" he asked. "I'd like to know where it's all heading. Nothing we do is *wrong* any more! I don't know whether that's bad or good, but it makes me worry. Things are so good we've lost our sense of appreciation. We've got everything."

We went inside and met Frances, his handsome blonde wife, whose father and brother were both mayor of Perth at some point, and their four children, aged eight to 24.

Frances told me Perthites were conservative—"It takes 25 years before you're considered one."

Eddie said they still had hillbilly-like feuds in the area but that they mostly shot each other's cattle.

Back at the hotel, there was a short conversation with barkeeper Hugh McDougall, 21, a hotel-administration student in Toronto. He had red hair, sideburns, and a moustache.

"Perth's dead and opinionated," said Hugh, a native. "A kind of Peyton Place. It's made up of old families and if you're not one of them you're out. Its greatest export is young people. They go away to school and they don't come back."

Hugh's worry was Americanization. "I don't want to be an American, but we're heading that way. I'm a Canadian. And I don't want president Nixon telling me what to do and sending me to war. I don't want that US 'feeling,' the prejudice, and tenseness, coming here."

He made the point that most Canadian kids could probably name ten American presidents, but how many prime ministers could they come up with?

I watched Fred Dixon belting it out for a while and then had a chat with John T. Ford, 79, retired 14 years from Eaton's mail-order office in Toronto. A resident of the hotel, he was reading the papers in a rocking chair in the lobby. He wore white socks and slippers. He didn't look his age.

"Maybe I should carry my birth certificate!" he said.

Ford came to Perth because his daughter lives there and because Toronto was getting too noisy. He said he read the *Globe and Mail* and *Ottawa Journal* every day, and the local papers. The rest of the time he spent visiting sick friends, watching hockey, and at the senior citizen's club. Canada was the nicest country "of the lot" to live in, but the "junk" on TV bothered him.

Also: "The laws are too lax. Used to be if you touched a cop you got two years. Nowadays they get a slap on the wrist and are sent home."

He wore a Great-War veteran's pin on his lapel. "There aren't many of us left," he said. "The average age is 75....Buried one yesterday."

What did he miss most?

"My wife," said Ford. "She passed away just before I retired."

Some 40 miles southwest of Quebec City, 11 miles along a country road running east out of Deschaillons, a village on the south shore of the St Lawrence River, there was a small eating place recommended because it possessed "the spirit of the family." It stood alone amid fields and bush—the nearest hamlet, Villeroy, was four miles away—and its steamy interior featured worn linoleum floors, a stovepipe suspended by wires running the length of the ceiling, green leatherette stools around a vinyl counter, seven tables with red-checkered cloths, and the owner's wife, Mariette Samson, in pink hot pants.

A wedding party had stopped in for beer and fried chicken, so Mme Samson didn't have much time to talk. She was a pretty woman, with dimples, brown hair piled high, and face glowing from the heat. She was from Villeroy; her husband, the cook, from Notre Dame de Lourdes, another nearby hamlet.

She would just as soon not discuss separatism. "I don't know enough about it," she said. "Anyway, I'm home everywhere. I have no nationality."

What really worried her was that, "People demand more and more but give less and less. Big salaries, yes, but no work. When I was 16," she said, "I did everything to make a living. Now everybody waits for Pierre Jean-Jacques [the government] to help."

Her mother-in-law, however, was not one of those. She died last year at 67. She had had 23 children including three sets of twins. In the winter of 1934, six days after the birth of the second set of twins, fire broke out in her farm home around midnight. She had put one of the babies on the kitchen table and *thought* she had placed the other next to it. Grabbing both she ran. But outside she found herself clutching one baby and a cushion. So one of the sons fought his way back in and got the other twin. There were only seven children then and the family spent the winter in a tent.

At the next table, truck driver Maurice Labbé, 56, sat nodding. A native of Notre Dame de Lourdes, he had heard the story before. He wanted to get back to economics.

"They say we are the richest country," he said, "yet we cannot survive in it. Something is wrong. I believe this is due to bad administration which started a long time ago. There must be some solution...but I don't have it."

His friend, Charles Auguste Côte, 38, a furniture maker, joined in. Also a lifelong resident of the area, he mentioned that he and his wife and another couple had crossed Canada by car the year before. Only one of them spoke a little English, yet everybody everywhere had been friendly and helpful. "But it was lonely, too," he said. "To drive hundreds of miles and not meet a soul who could speak French."

Mme Samson suggested I meet her uncle, M. Bédard, a taxi driver, who lived next door, and maybe later, in Notre Dame de Lourdes, speak to the priest, M. le Curé Olivier Patenaude.

Bédard's tiny wooden house was straight out of a fairy tale book—an improbable collection of turrets, verandas, shutters, and bits of things jutting out as decoration, all in the wildest colours and fabricated from old school benches, sewing machines, piano legs, and what not.

In the front yard, his pride and joy was a small wooden church built to scale. It was embellished with a huge star of ladies' hat pins, a silver car grill, and doors and windows cut from a yellow plastic hamper and looking just like stained glass.

Bédard, 65, a large, heavy man, was a bachelor. He'd been in the taxi business 32 years, but it wasn't good; people couldn't afford him. He had never been outside Quebec except once to visit a brother in Kansas. Now he wasn't really interested in travel any more. He preferred to stay at home and work on his house and cook his favourite dishes—potatoes, salted pork and beans, pancakes, and pea soup. Separatism—"I don't know enough about it"—was not a subject of much interest. This is what he felt bad about: "Life is not the same as it was because people don't get along any more. There's too much money and not enough done to earn it. People are getting lazier...."

Curé Olivier Patenaude, a friendly, hospitable man of 62, was pleased to speak English. "I get to use it so seldom here," he said.

Three years before, he had been transferred, after 27 years of service near Thetford Mines, Quebec, to take over the parishes of Villeroy and Notre Dame de Lourdes—some 290 families. Whatever time he had free he spent reading (eight English magazines and newspapers, and a dozen French ones), listening to opera, and watching hockey on TV. From the order of the Brothers of the Holy Cross he had served with the Canadian army for five years and had been in Korea. He had also studied theology for a year in Paris.

"My big topic for sermons," he said, "is the necessity to be *real* Christians. Don't be half a Christian. Love God and your neighbours. I read the Bible again and again."

He left his sitting room for a moment and returned with a much-handled Bible full of margin notes. "I had this as a student. It's an instrument for me, like a carpenter's tool.

"In my last sermon I warned them of the situation in Quebec. I said: 'Before the end of the year we will see blood flow again. We will have another October crisis. Strikes are no good. Hotheads will turn others. We are on a volcano! Pray to God...for we will have trouble.'"

<hr/>

It snowed when the plane took off from Quebec, and it snowed landing in Moncton. The airport rent-a-car clerk said six inches was forecast. She also said that if I was just going to tool around in New Brunswick, why didn't I stop off in her hometown of Shediak, Lobster Capital of the World. Why not?

In winter, Shediak, 16 miles northeast of Moncton, shelters perhaps 2,500 people and it's quiet. But there are about 3,000 cottages in the area and in summer the population soars to 20,000. It's the lobster and beaches that bring them in.

Mme Yvonne Hébert, a short, attractive French Canadian, and part owner of the 4-Seasons Motel and Restaurant, said the tourists came from everywhere, "Montreal, Oklahoma, Ontario."

She had worked in restaurants, in Prince Edward Island and Halifax, she said, since she was 16. "In Halifax it was rush, rush, rush. You didn't get to know the customer. Here you get to know the customer. I like it. It's peaceful. The neighbours are friendly. When I went to the hospital—woman trouble—everybody sent me cards."

I went back to my motel room, turned on the TV, and there was the indestructible Don Messer. And Margo and Charlie, too.

Mme Hébert had spoken highly of Joseph Landry, businessman and former mayor of Shediac. I met him and his wife,

Bertha, who owns a hairdresser's shop, later that Saturday evening. They invited me along to a dance at the 325-member social club named after Colonel Bois Hébert who fought a battle at Shediac around 1652.

"The most threatening thing in this country is strikes," said Landry. "To my mind they're spearheaded by communism. We had one at the old people's home and Bertha worked there five weeks straight through."

"I fed and bathed them," said Bertha. "And I gave them their pills, took them for walks, and gave them manicures."

Landry was proud of Shediac. "People live here in total harmony," he said. "You can go visiting without an appointment. The other day we built a skating rink right out on the street....You can do that in a small place."

In the terminal waiting for the ferry to Prince Edward Island, I saw a girl get up from the purple plastic benches with "Keep on Trucking" stitched on the seat of her jeans. Ed MacLaren, 24, a business administration student in Charlottetown, saw it at the same time, so we got to talking.

"The Maritimes feel so cut off from Canada," he said, "that it doesn't matter much what happens there. We blank it out. I, personally, can't wait to get out, and go and live in Calgary. A lot of Islanders live there. Our biggest problem, actually, is losing our young people. There's nothing to keep them here.

"A 'Maritimes union' might be a good thing. But it'll probably never happen. First thing they wouldn't be able to agree on would be where to have the capital."

Aboard the ferry cutting through wicked-looking ice floes, Ed said hello by first name to at least 20 of the 150-odd passengers. Occasionally, people nodded to me, too.

In Bedeque, a tiny place in the gentle country between Port Borden and Summerside, I met two retired ladies named Eleanor Wheler and Elaine Harrison. Eleanor said that she had been a nurse and came to PEI 27 years ago; Elaine mentioned she had been a teacher of English, Latin, and German and had settled

35 years before. They lived in a tiny, two-storey house crammed with books, magazines, paintings, wood-burning stoves, two dogs, and 14 cats. In summer they lived in a bungalow six miles away on the beach. They painted, read, gardened, took walks, went to concerts, hooked rugs, and talked.

"What I'm fed up with," said Elaine, the more forceful of the two, "are all the development plans in this country! They're destroying the little villages; destroying good and valid ways of life."

"Yes," said Eleanor in her more quiet way, "we're growing more and more concerned about the despoiling...."

"The Maritimes, for instance," Elaine boomed, "are being brainwashed. They say that we're poor and backward and under-privileged. Nonsense! We are *not!*"

They served tea and sliced bread with butter, and fruitcake.

"We're still considered foreigners here by some people," said Eleanor, smiling, "We're 'from away.'"

The ladies refused to be photographed, but I was welcome back any time.

On the nine-mile return trip to New Brunswick, I heard a woman say to a friend:

"I don't know what it is, but when I come back from the Island, I feel so rested."

●━◆━●

The PEI ladies' quiet but definite refusal to be photographed I encountered again in Stewiacke (pop. 982), about 18 miles south of Truro, Nova Scotia. It was beginning to look as if Maritimers were either more shy, more modest, or set more store on privacy than other Canadians.

Mrs Grace McLennan, the town clerk refused; so did Edmund Crowe, a columnist with *The Truro Daily News* and author of the town's 136-page history; the young police chief, Harold MacKenzie; and deputy clerk Mrs Merna Robinson, née Smith, sister of G.I. Smith, the province's former premier.

On the edge of Stewiacke—which means "winding river" in Mi'kmaq—was this sign: YOU ARE NOW EXACTLY HALFWAY

BETWEEN THE EQUATOR AND THE NORTH POLE. It seemed a good reason to stop.

Mrs McLennan was in her office in the town hall, a square, two-storey wooden structure, which also functions as fire hall, police station, library, and magistrate's court. Eventually, the others showed up there as well.

Mrs McLennan said the town had 10.5 miles of street, seven of them paved.

The reason she lived in a little place, she said, was because, "You're freer than in the city, and it's quiet. We don't want to grow too much. We're already lacking services and houses."

"The *worst* a small town can do," said writer Crowe, aged 73, "is to push for growth and development. What for? We have the best fishing here, the best skating."

"I like it here just as it is," said police chief MacKenzie, who came from Halifax. "I wouldn't ever want to live in the city again. Here you can just jump on your snowmobile whenever you want."

"I wouldn't want to see it grow too big," said Mrs Robinson.

That evening I joined Crowe, in his reporter capacity, and attended magistrate's court. At 7 PM sharp, the Mountie got up and said. "Stand please. I declare this court open in the name of the Queen!"

There were 16 cases of traffic offences and liquor abuse. Everybody pleaded guilty, and the magistrate said thank you each time he was paid. It took less than an hour. Occasionally, Crowe winked at me. There was something pleasant in a sleepy way about Stewiacke that could become infectious.

——◆———

Petty Harbour (pop. 842) is only about 12 miles south of St John's. It is the most easterly tip of North America—1,780 miles of Atlantic Ocean separate it from Cape Clare, Ireland. Its little wooden houses cling to rocky hills and look down on a small, quiet bay. You can drive in and around its two or three narrow streets on a weekday and not meet a soul, except if school's out. It once lived entirely off fishing, but now many of the residents work in St John's and commute.

Like Edgar Butler, 28. He said he was a car salesman in the city, though he wasn't working then because of an illness that makes talking difficult for him. He invited me up to his mother-in-law's, Mrs Mildred Chafe.

She was sitting by the kitchen window darning socks. Her husband, she told me, was a boilermaker with the railroad. "But we've always lived here," she said. "We wouldn't like the city to live in. And Petty Harbour's really beautiful in the fall.

"You see, you don't make so many friends in the city," she explained. "If you're sick or in trouble here, people do what they can for you."

I asked a stock question.

"We've got no worries," she said. "A little sickness, but who doesn't? There's plenty to eat, and we've got a dollar when we want it."

Mother of five children and grandmother to ten, she said that today it was more trouble to raise her youngest grandchild than her own five combined. She blamed a lot of it on bad TV programs.

In her free time, she said, she played bingo or cards, had tea with her women's club, and worked for the church. "I love going to church," Mrs Chafe said. "On Sunday I might go three times. What's the sense of paying a clergyman if you don't go and listen to him?"

Mrs Chafe would not have her picture taken.

Edgar and I went out so I could explore a little more. On a road leading out of the village along the water, we met Fred Stack and Robert Clark. They sat in a car scanning the ocean with binoculars. They were the only other adults I saw in Petty Harbour.

Fred, 55, was a firefighter in St John's and Robert, 65, a highway labourer. Both were born and raised in the place. Fred was the more talkative of the two, but neither volunteered very much.

"Don't like city life," said Fred. "Here I've got all the freedom I want. I wouldn't swap here for Toronto, Montreal, or Quebec."

"Never been anywhere else," said Robert. "Love it here."

Fred picked up the binoculars and watched a little boat puffing out of Petty Harbour into the bay. "He's going duck hunting," he said.

"I don't see any," I said.

"There's billions out there," said Fred. "Salt-water ducks."

"Are they good to eat?" I asked.

"Sure," said Robert, speaking for the second and last time.

The four of us looked out over the water, at the boat, at some gulls swooping. We didn't have anything more to say. I became conscious of the stillness.

"I'd like to come back here," I said, "but stay a while. Walk around."

An innocuous enough thing to say. But the three seemed primed for it. Robert's rough, red face broke into a grin and so did Edgar's. They grinned and nodded their heads. Fred didn't do that. He thumped the wheel of the car.

"That's *it*, you see!" he almost shouted. "That's *it*. You want to come back and walk around!"

Credits

The following are all from *Weekend Magazine*, 1969–1973.

1. "The Old Ways Are Fading Away." *XIX, 43, 25 Oct 1969. p. 10.*

2. Few and Free. *XXIII, 32, 11 Aug 1973. p. 2.*

3. Where They Work Only Two Months a Year. *XXIII, 15, 14 Apr 1973. p. 2.*

4. "You Spend Your Life on Horses Who Want Nothing More Than to Get You Off." *XXIII, 1, 6 Jan 1973. p. 16.*

5. "Somebody From a Big Family Knows Better How to Live Together." *XX, 12, 18 Mar 1972. p. 2.*

6. Fastest Bar in the East. *XIX, 29, 19 Jul 1969. p. 16.*

7. What Have We Done for the Indians in Stony Rapids? [No Mail for Roderick Yooya] *XX, 24, 13 Jun 1970. p. 13.*

8. A Book Lover's Bookstore. *XX, 6, 7 Feb 1970. p. 12.*

9. "Fish Aren't Born to Feel Sorry For." *XX, 12, 21 Mar 1970. p. 11.*

10. "The Mountain Belongs to the Bums." *XXIII, 9, 3 Mar 1973. p. 6.*

11. "There's a Deep Hunger Today for the Simple Word of God." *XXI, 32, 7 Aug 1971. p. 4.*

12. "What Suffering and Death That Light Has Averted." *XXII, 25, 17 Jun 1972. p. 2.*

13. "A 'Good' Wolf Is a Dead Wolf." *XXI, 17, 24 Apr 1971. p. 4.*

14. Printer's Ink Is in His Veins and All Over His Shirt. *XXIII, 2, 13 Jan 1973. p. 16.*

15. "Not in Our Lifetime, or Our Children's Lifetime, Will We See the End of This Pollution." *XX, 28, 11 Jul 1970. p. 4.*

16. Of Pies and Chips and Pillow Slips and Cabbages and Things. *XXII, 48, 25 Nov 1972. p. 2.*

17. The Only Human Tracks for Miles Around. *XXIII, 20, 19 May 1973. p. 2.*

18. Seventy Million Canadians Can't All Be Wrong. *XX, 49, 5 Dec 1970. p. 8.*

19. Maintenance of Law and Order—and Double Parking. *XXII, 33, 12 Aug 1972. p. 8.*

20. At the Snuff of a Candle, Dracula Appears. *XXIII, 52, 29 Dec 1973. p. 12.*

21. A Man in the Middle of Misery. *XXI, 34, 21 Aug 1971. p. 4.*

22. Travels Through a Winter Country. *XXII, 27, 1 Jul 1972. p. 2.*